AF819783

ORGANIZATION AND ADMINISTRATION IN PHYSICAL EDUCATION & SPORTS

DR. JAWAID ALI

KHEL SAHITYA KENDRA
7/26, Ansari Road, Daryaganj,
New Delhi-110002

Published by:
KHEL SAHITYA KENDRA
7/26, Ansari Road, Darya Ganj, New Delhi-110002
Ph.: (O) 011-65190343, 43551324, 42564726
(M) 9811088729, (Fax) 011-42564726
(Res.) 47091605
E-mail: khelsahitya1@rediffmail.com
Web: www.khelsahitya.com

© 2026 Author

ISBN : 978-81-7524-287-6

PRINTED IN INDIA 2026

All Rights Reserved.
No part of this publication may be stored in a retrieval system, transmitted or reproduced in any way, including but not limited to photocopy, photograph, magnetic or other record, without the prior agreement and written permission of the publisher.

Printed by:
S.K. OFFSET PRINTERS,
Delhi

Price: Rs. 900/-

PROF. AJMER SINGH
Arjuna Awardee
Olympian & Asian Games Gold Medalist

1470, Sector 49-B, Chandigarh
Ph.: 0172-634026

FOREWORD

There is acute scarcity of good indigenous literature in the field of physical education and sports in our country. People in the profession had been depending on books written by foreigners, which are very costly. Education institutions do not have so much funds to afford these books, hence are deprived of it. Moreover the material in foreign books is not in consonance with our facilities, and curriculum in schools and colleges.

I am happy to know that Dr. Jawaid Ali Khan has taken the initiative and pains to write this book "Organization and Administration in Physical Education and Sports". The book deals with all the processes and procedures for running the physical education programme in our education institutions.

Since it provides insight to all the important aspects of physical education curriculum, I am sure the book will prove to be a boon for affective implementation of the programmes. All concerned – teachers, students, coaches, administrators, organizers – will be benefited by valuable information contained in this book.

Prof. Ajmer Singh
Former Vice-Chancellor
Lakshmi Bai National Institute of
Physical Education (Deemed University)
GWALIOR

Preface

Physical education is one of the important academic disciplines that involves both theoretical and practical instructions. It is observed that in educational institutions physical education is not accorded its due status almost at all levels. It causes lopsided personality development of youth. Effective organization and skillful administration are the real needs of contemporary physical education, health care and recreation programmes in our country. A systematic body of knowledge is required in order to groom the young leaders for becoming able administrators of physical education. Creative leadership and competent management are dependable pillars on which to build a strong base of physical education. Leaders of physical education must know how to work within the framework of an organization under the supervision of an administrator.

The book includes all those contents that are necessary to better prepare future administrators and to fill the void in the area of physical education. I am confident that this book will be of real assistance to teachers, administrators and students of physical education.

I am greatly indebted to all those who have motivated me for bringing out the present text. I sincerely thank to my wife and children for being source of inspiration and also tolerating my prolong absence from family affairs.

—Dr. Jawaid Ali

Contents

1

Basic Notion of Physical Education and Sports

In order to proceed efficiently and with dispatch toward any goal it is essential that the goal be known. Furthermore, attainment which will be educationally satisfactory is only possible if the end to be gained is worthy; it is not sufficient to attain just any goal. Consequently, the physical educator, in addition to having adequate aims, must have worthwhile objectives and know how to cause them to be achieved. Except for an illustration which points out the relationship of the pursuit of objectives to instruction centred in an activity class, the matter of attainment will be considered in subsequent. This presentation of objective specifically excludes achievement standards in physical education program activities as well as consideration of equipment, staff, and methods of organization and administration, since those aspects are not considered "objectives." They are treated under other headings.

Method of Attack

In developing adequate aims and objectives a comprehensive list of aims, objectives, sub-objectives, and, in some cases, even items was compiled and classified, with the various categories under the respective headings toward the attainment of which they could be expected to make a significant contribution. The objectives and sub-objectives were subjected in turn to criteria developed from the related fields and the goals of education and then notated as to whether they satisfied or failed to satisfy the condition stated in each criterion or goal. It became apparent that inclusion of sub-objectives and items would add greatly to detail and confusion rather than to clarity. Consequently, the objectives with the aims under which they appear were used. Those judged as meeting the criteria and goals adequately are listed as the aims and objectives of physical education. The objectives selected are ranked in two groups: those most worthy of general pursuit and those less worthy of general pursuit, according to the number of criteria and goals they meet satisfactorily.

Definition of Terms

Physical education is considered as that part of all education which proceeds by means of, or predominantly through, physical activity. Aim is used to denote a general purpose. It is a term used for a general category under which several objectives appear, for example, development of personality. Objectives are practical, more nearly attainable, major steps or points of significance toward realization of aims, such as attainment of sportsmanship or self-control. Sub-objectives are points to be attained in reaching an objective, such as controlling anger. Items are component parts of a sub-objective, such as controlling anger when the official calls a foul on one.

Fundamental Limitations of Objectives

Objectives are to apply at eh most suitable time. It is apparent that not all objectives apply equally to all ages of a student or to all students. The first-grade pupil should not be expected to concentrate on teamwork, which, however, is one of the important sub-objectives for the high school group. Increases self-expression need not be stressed in the student who is already a nuisance because of an overdeveloped urge to be a performer, both vocally and physically. However, in the case of the overtimid child a greater desire for expression is needed. Individual differences must be considered but cannot be provided for in detail in setting up general objectives, for that would require a set of objectives for each individual. Actually, good instruction varies enough from the established objectives to make the desirable adjustments in practice, even though the general setup cannot provide a list for each student.

A useful distinction has been pointed out by many authors between objectives to be definitely pursued now, those that are also valuable but incidental to the main drive at present, and those that will be of value later on. Improvement of co-ordination is one of the first type. During the time that instruction is being offered in skills that will help to improve co-ordination, the individual might well be instructed in social values, such as sportsmanship and self-control. By proper selection of activity it is possible to build toward a more remote objective, that of development of a leisure-time activity. In teaching the game of tennis, a physical activity, the three objectives above, along with many others, should prevail in the mind of the instructor. As the student is learning eye-hand co-ordination in striking the ball, he can very well learn to refrain from objecting to decisions of those officiating at the practice games and from displaying temper at the strokes he misses. As he improves his game he is developing a leisure-time activity for the present and for later years. The attainment of many objectives, even of different types, proceeds concurrently. Since certain goals may be decidedly worth attaining in childhood, others later on, and still others in adult life, the objectives here considered are judged on the basis of the time when they apply best-in the instance of their optimum value. Any objective that does not apply at all in school, needs to have a very strong case made for it in order to justify its pursuit there, and those objectives that apply very well in school should be retained unless an extremely strong case can be built against them on other grounds.

It must be remembered that the objectives listed are not supposed to be attained entirely through physical education. Physical education is considered as contributing only in part to them. In the matter of normal growth and development, which certainly is one concern of physical education, many other influences than those brought to bear in a physical education class are very important. Sleep, rest, sanitary conditions at home and at school, occupation before and after school, the amount and kind of food, and inheritance set the rate and direction very largely. Physical education can only do the best possible under the limitations placed upon it in this and other possible under the limitations placed upon it in this and other possible under the limitations placed upon it in this and other respects. In some cases greater opportunity for service is provided because of proportionately grater lack in the remainder of the child's environment. Physical education, then, is one of the influences contributing to the objectives set up; it could not be otherwise, since the individual is touched only at intervals and often for only short periods, by organized physical education in schools.

Zoological Criteria

A. The objectives and their attainment should fit in with nature's plan concerning the physical organism.

1. The objectives should stress action of the large muscles since phylogenic development of the large-muscle groups furnished the incentive and reason for development of the other organic systems.

i. During ontogenetic development a large amount of exercise of these groups is essential to healthy functioning of other organs.

ii. The other systems still depend upon action of those same muscle groups for proper functioning during adult life.

2. The objectives should stress proper organic functioning since proper muscular functioning depends upon proper organic functioning which it stimulates.

3. The objectives should provide opportunity to work off the internal secretions produced during strong emotional states, since when strong emotions are aroused, and they often are in youth, opportunity to express them in action benefits the body and lack of such expression harms it.

4. Probably the objective should not be conducive to abnormal development of any body part, since there is danger in greatly exceeding normal development of any body part.

A. The attained objective should be conducive to success in group living. It should contribute to success in a society organized in such a way as ours.

1. The objective should fit in with the predominant social restraints.

2. The objective should emphasize the character traits accepted as valuable in our society.

3. The objectives should emphasize the physical traits accepted as valuable in our society.

4. The objective should emphasize the mental traits accepted as valuable in America.

5. Other things being equal, those objectives that can be attained through social contacts in physical education are to be preferred.

<u>Psychological Criteria</u>

I. The objective to be of value must be attainable through some mechanism with which the human body is provided.

II. The objective to be of value must be such that progress toward its attainment is possible.

III. The objective will be attained more readily if the steps in its attainment are interesting.

IV. The objective will be attained more readily if provision can be made for correct repetition of the elements that comprise it. Correct practice includes:

A. Avoidance of errors.

B. Clear identification of connections to be made.

C. Provision for maturation.

D. Proper fusion of the elements.

V. The objective will be attained more readily if practice of the elements comprising it is satisfying. Satisfying. Satisfaction is increased by:

A. Facility of tie-up with intensive universal drives.

B. Presence of favourable and absence of contrary emotional drives.

C. Clear conception and acceptance of the purpose.

D. Practice in the absence of marked fatigue.

VI. The objective will be attained more readily if it is possible to take into account and provide for individual differences in establishing the elements of which it is comprised.

VII. The objective will be attained more readily if certain elements of it can be selected and stressed at favourable times.

Transfer Criteria

I. The objective will be of greater value if it is such that provision can be made for efficient transfer to other situations.

A. Generalization that have future as well as present carry-over value should be used as basis of transfer.

B. Ideas, skills, habits, and attitudes may well be included as of transfer value.

C. Possible negative transfers should be avoided.

D. The more intense the situation the better the transfer possibilities.

A corollary statement of the major criterion of transfer might well be added in conclusion: the unit of transfer should not be a minute detail or an extremely complex group of generalizations but a simple generalization of a group of details.

Educational Criterion and Goals

I. The objectives must fit in with the generally accepted aims or goals of education. The question asked of all objective and sub-objectives concerning each of the following seven goals is: Does ... assist in attaining this goal?

A. Health.

B. Command of fundamental processes.

C. Worthy home membership

D. Vocational preparation.

E. Citizenship preparation.

F. Worthy use of leisure time.

G. Development of ethical character.

The Use of Aims and Objectives

The pupil attainment aims and objectives are presented as standards of achievement toward which the instructor can direct the efforts of the students. It is not recommended that this be done by constantly calling the pupil's attention to the goals to be achieved, but instead by so arranging the instructional situation that from the content, the atmosphere, and the methods used the student will actually pursue the desired objectives. Since most youngsters participate in activities or play the games for the fun of it, and play with very little enthusiasm unless it is fun, they do not wish to be bothered by having repeated to them a set of aims and objectives toward which the instructor expects them to be working; nor do they care to spend their activity periods philosophizing about objectives. However, if the situation is set up and managed in such a way that it is more fun for the students to pursue the desired goals than it is for them to pursue less desirable ends, then the participants will naturally follow the pattern that provides greater enjoyment and thus pursue sound aims and objectives of physical education. The great value of aims and objectives is not just that they are stated and accepted but that are pursued and lived out in action. Consequently, attention needs to be given to the matter of putting them in operation.

The point can be illustrated in connection with a junior high school physical education program. A great number of activities should be included in the program. From among them this representative group will be used: basketball, folk dancing, stunts, and track and field. These may well be the activities for boys and girls for one semester. The objectives should be kept in mind as the staff or the individual teacher plans the program for the semester. The instructor will check through the objectives and plan points of emphasis where the various objectives can receive particular attention, keeping in mind that many of the objectives are pursued at the same time. Knowing that the students will achieve the objectives more generally if the instructor lives or practices them, each teacher will demonstrate them in attitude and action starting, with the first meeting of the class. For instance, at the first meeting of the class at the beginning of the spring semester, the activity to be considered is basketball. If this is a new class for the instructor, there will be among other things roll taking, preliminary getting acquainted with each other, some instructions concerning procedures, probably locker assignment, and appointments for medical exams for any who need one at this time. In this first organizing meeting pursuit of the objectives should be put into operation by the instructor, especially through demonstrating them by the way things are done. Positive active qualities and qualities of efficiency should be much in evidence. This will make for well-organized procedure and doing things with dispatch, as contrasted to disorganization and hesitation. Some knowledge should be dispensed concerning proper health procedure as related to physical exercise. This may be done in the from of advice concerning warm-up, taking showers, wearing proper activity clothes, and excuses from activity when ill with a cold.

The instructor can demonstrate, among other qualities, sociability and leadership in the manner used in dealing with the students. If class leaders are to be used, the method of selection can be put into operation. By providing summary essentials of playing rules the process of attaining knowledge of rules can get underway. At the second meeting when the class is dressed for activity the objectives listed above are pursued along with several additional ones among which are samplings of the various objectives under skills and abilities aim. There will be development of psychomotor skills and proper development of special sense with body movement in eye-hand co-ordination as well as in the touch and feel of the ball in catching, passing, and shooting. Certainly there will be development of sills common to America generally, for basketball is truly an American game. There will be further development of natural racial activities in throwing, jumping, running, and dodging, and, of course, excellent opportunities to develop general bodily control in the pivoting, stopping, starting, and changing of direction in the drills. Here, too, is to be found preparation for leisure time, for basketball is one of the major leisure-time activities for our young people. The process of improving morale through improving the body will also get underway as the activity adds to the conditioning of the participant. In this first activity meeting and in subsequent class sessions, the interest in and the fun of playing the game will help eliminate or diminish worry through appropriate interest in physical activity in that the participant will get lost in the game-that is, get lost from worries and problems which were built up in other areas. There will also be an increase in general neural vigour, for neural vigour is increased through action of the large-muscle groups. Strong nerves are based on strong muscles, which are developed through adequate exercise. Basketball provides background preparation for spending a portion of one's leisure time in an enjoyable physical activity, for basketball is a popular game, which, like other games, is enjoyable only if enough ability is developed to perform the various skills acceptably.

A well-taught class will do this. Maintaining a clean activity area, clean uniforms, and in taking a shower after exercise, acquiring the habit of cleanliness is developed. From the purely physical angle basketball participation makes a definite contribution to development of endurance and strength. This presupposes a well-conducted class wherein all able students get a good work-out each class period. This will be enhanced by an adequate supply of balls and maximum use of facilities.

Along with the personality objectives presented above, sportsmanship, self-control, and positive mental qualities are developed in the give and take and the enthusiasm and drive necessary in playing the game. Basketball and the other activities suggested make their contribution, although but a minor one, to normal growth and development and sound and proper functioning of the students. As pointed out earlier, physical activity is only one of the contribution factors to these two objectives, and, since only a small percentage of the total physical activity of junior high school students is gained in physical education classes, the contribution to the objectives must of necessity be limited.

It is evident that knowledge of techniques and methods should be gained by all who participate in a well-taught class. As the other activities listed for the semester are taught the same objectives as those mentioned for basketball are pursued. Some activities lend themselves to the emphasis of certain objectives more readily than others do. There is more emphasis on developing co-ordination of the sense of hearing with bodily movements in folk dancing, for example, than there is in stunts; there is also greater opportunity to prepare for use of leisure time than there is in track and field.

However, a track meet with another school can make a greater contribution to the promotion of school spirit than can a folk dance festival, which, in turn, can contribute successfully to social co-operation. Such objectives as promotion of school spirit, presenting interesting performances or shows, and advertising the school are pursued quite generally during the preparation for and presentation of activities for parents' night and other exhibitions. Folk dances, stunts, demonstrations of basketball games, and basketball lead-up games are useful units of such performances. Although these performances are not give during physical education class meetings, the basic skills and general preparation are taught and developed in connection with class work. By the manner in which the class is taught, by the guidance provided by the instructor, and by the practices and attitude of the instructor some of the students should discover the value of establishing a schedule of daily activities that fit their own beings. Since this is a difficult problem for many adults as well as students, it is not proposed that participation in a physical education class will bring about a revolution in the lives of the students, but rather that some progress can be made in this area if the class is well conducted.

Although first aid should probably be taught in a course designed especially for that purpose, the instructor can demonstrate correct first-aid practices as he meets the first-aid problems that arise in his activity class from time to time. He may even use such first-aid situations to point out some of the undesirable procedures that should be avoided. The above illustrations present bout a brief account of some of the ways that objectives are related to the activities which contribute to their attainment.

They are presented for the use of those who might be concerned about just how the objectives listed tie in with actual class instruction. With other age groups, both younger and older, the different objectives will be given varying emphasis and attention. Individual instructors will also wish to place different emphasis on the various objectives. However, pursuit of all of the objectives should be practised at all age levels.

The Aims and Objectives of Physical Education

These are the aims and objectives of physical education, classified into two groups on the basis of worthiness of general pursuit.

Those most worthy of general pursuit include:

1. Mental hygiene aim

Eliminating or diminishing worry and stress, through developing appropriate interests and habits of engaging in exercise and sports.

Increasing general neural vigour.

2. Skills and abilities aim

• Development of proper co-ordination of special senses with body movement.

• Development of psychomotor skills.

• Development of skills related to natural, racial activities.

• Development of general bodily control.

• Development of skills common to America generally

and to one's own locality particularly.

3. Cultural aim

- Development of understanding and appreciation of the techniques and strategies of sports.
- Preparation for leisure time.
- Improvement of morale through improving body.

4. Purely physical aim

- To assist in the development of endurance sufficient to meet the needs of the stress of life and a little bit more.
- To assist in developing strength enough to do normal life tasks without undue strain.
- To assist in providing for normal growth and development.

5. Desirable habits aim

- Establishment of a schedule of daily activities that fits one's own being.
- Acquiring the habit of habits of spending a portion of one's leisure time in enjoyable physical activity.
- Acquiring the habit of cleanliness.

6. Personality aim

- Attainment of sportsmanship.
- Attainment of self-control.
- Attainment of social co-operation.
- Attainment of qualities of efficiency.
- Attainment of sociability.
- Attainment of leadership.

- Attainment of positive active qualities.
- Attainment of positive mental qualities.

7. Prestige aim

- Promotion of school spirit.

8. Applied knowledge aim

Attainment of knowledge of proper health procedure as related to physical exercise.

Those less worthy of general pursuit are:

1. Applied knowledge aim

Attainment of knowledge of techniques and methods.

Attainment of knowledge or rules.

Attainment of knowledge of first aid.

2. Purely physical aim

To assist in developing and maintaining sound and proper functioning.

3. Prestige aim

Presenting interesting performances or shows.

Advertising school or institution.

2

The Physical Education Plant

There are very few principles of physical education administration that have been less adequately applied than have those that deal with the planning and construction of buildings to house the program. The large number of inadequate physical education buildings, even on university campuses, is material evidence of this fact. Several factors have contributed to this condition. One of most significant has been the practice of copying a building in a neighbouring city or state, mistakes and good points alike. This practice has been employed because it has proved to be temporarily less troublesome than making a survey of local conditions, a study of building construction, and evaluating the results by a sound educational philosophy, before starting to build. Another factor has been a change in educational philosophy and a consequent shift in emphasis from a formal to a more natural activity program.

The newer program demands more and different activity rooms, which tends to make the older type of plant obsolete. In some situations there has been an unwillingness on the part of those in authority to seek and utilize the advice of informed staff members, and in others physical education people have proved unable to advise judiciously when consulted. Wise and efficient planning and construction of a physical education plant can obviate many administrative, financial, and functional difficulties.

A few examples of this are presented here and again later, since they deserve to be emphasized by repetition. Direct stairs from locker rooms to gym floor and a small visitors' balcony will eliminate the problem of keeping students in street shoes off the gym floor; well-placed activity room will make supervision relatively easy; properly recessed radiators will reduce the number of accidents; reduction of unnecessary hall space will save money; properly placed drinking fountains and lavatories will make the building a more efficient service unit; properly sloped cement floors will be easier to clean; a sloping roof will shed water much better than a flat one; louvre type windows will provide good ventilation, even in rainy weather; cement locker bases will make the cleaning of the locker room easier; and the concentration of showers; lavatories, and drinking fountains in a comparatively small area will reduce the plumbing bill. Any effort spent in planning will pay large dividends in the future to those who are responsible for the physical education unit. It is not enough to hire an architect and leave all matters of arrangement to him, for he does not have the background or philosophy which the competent physical educator has.

The one who is to plan an efficient unit must understand the program it is to use. Certainly an architect is necessary, but he must be guided in order that the finished building may be an adequate service unit as well as a thing of beauty. We have probably reached a point in the construction of school buildings where the public is going to be more and more critical of the method by which its tax money is spent. This means that the builder to tomorrow will need to plan very carefully in order that he may provide an efficient physical education unit with the some what limited funds available.

Location of Building—for small communities this is determined at the time the site of the school is selected, for there is often but one building to house the entire school. For somewhat larger schools, where the buildings must all be placed in a limited area, the matter of placement of the physical education building is of relatively small significance; but for large schools, especially colleges and universities, the location of the building or buildings often sets quite definitely the limits of their serviceability. At some universities the field house, physical education plant, or playing areas are so far removed from the major concentration of classrooms that in many instances students must rush to and from academic and activity classes.

This need to hurry tends to make physical education an unpleasant experience for the student. When the activity areas are far removed from the living quarters students who lack transportation are handicapped in their efforts to participate in intramural competition because it is a work-out to travel to and from the are. Since the participant must take two work-outs or none, quite number of them will choose none rather than two, especially on those occasions when the weather is bad or there are other events competing for their time. These absences can be a major cause of forfeiture of intramural contests, and the anticipation of the problems involved in travelling back and forth may account for failure to sign up for participation in the first place. Since the physical education plant is a service unit, it should be located in a pleasant environment on a properly drained site near the centre of the campus where all students may find it readily accessible when they have an hour or tow for physical activity. A well-constructed physical education plant does not mar a landscape, but instead enhances it. Beautiful grass and shrubs are poor substitutes for normal, healthy students in any case. If the school does not provide a convenient recreational unit, outside interests will replace recreation with commercialized amusement which is socially and financially less valuable.

Room Dimensions

The size, shape, and height of rooms will vary according to the purposes for which they are to be used; consequently, it is not possible to determine the optimum dimensions without knowing the local conditions which will affect them. However, there are general limits which should be observed, except in rate cases when some specific modifying factor dictates different proportions. In case of doubt moderation rather than extremism is a sound policy to follow in planning size of rooms. This is particularly true of size, since too large a room is proportionately more expensive in terms of service it can render per unit cost. There are but few occasions when such a room can be used to capacity, and all idle, enclosed space represents an unwarranted financial burden. Then, too, more teaching stations can be provided if the enclosed space is broken into smaller units. Except for ticket booths, toilets, closets, offices, and rooms of that type, very small rooms are not particularly serviceable, for they must, of necessity, remain idle much of the time. Those smaller than 12 by 15 feet are hard to justify.

The building should be constructed in such a way that it will contribute most to the entire educational system. Sliding walls will provide for varying room sizes. This point of view will limit extravagant expenditure of funds for construction of extra-large seating accommodations for basketball crowds, which will be needed on only a night or two a year when a particular rival plays on the home floor. The chief function of the plant should not be that of providing seats for spectators but of providing a laboratory for training citizens. Roll-away bleachers, which can be pushed back when not in use, thus leaving more space for activities, are strongly recommended instead of the old stationary bleachers. Odd-shaped, many-sided rooms with projections are costly to construct and are limited in their uses; consequently, they should be eliminated as much as possible in the planning. The main gymnasium room or basketball court should be approximately one and a half times as long as it is wide.

This shape lends itself well to use for common activities, and it can be spanned more economically than a square room of the same floor area. The smaller activity rooms and academic classrooms should be longer than they are wide with a ratio of about five to three-respectively. Each room should have sufficient height of ceiling to accommodate the activities which are to take place in it. Any additional height is unnecessary and costly, and any reduction in height cramps the activity program. Where basketball and similar games are to be played, the clearance from the floor to the ceiling should be 25 feet. Where there is a balcony, however, it may need to be 30 feet or higher. Locker, shower, and classrooms need not be more than 10 feet to 12 feet in height. Handball courts should be of regulation height. To admit sunlight and provide for diving, the ceiling above swimming pools should be 20 feet to 25 feet above the level of the floor around the pool.

Arrangement

It is in regard to arrangement that a great many mistakes in building planning are made, for a comparatively large share of planning has to do with the relationship of rooms to each other and the placement of the various service fixtures within the rooms. The placing of service fixtures will be considered under the discussion of each fixture. The following points should be kept in mind when considering the matter of correct room, hall, and stair arrangement within the building:

1. Place units that are to be used together close to each other.

(a) The medical supervisor's room should be adjacent to the locker room.

(b) The shower room should adjoin the locker room.

(c) The swimming pool should be close to the shower room.

(d) The supply and equipment room should be contiguous to the locker room.

(e) The storeroom should be conveniently near the supply room.

(f) The drying room should be near the equipment and shower rooms.

(g) The apparatus room should be adjacent to the gym floor and provided with large doors.

(h) The toilets and lavatories should be near the locker room.

(i) The director's office should be in a location convenient for supervision of activities.

(j) The waiting room should be close to the director's office.

(k) The janitor's room should be adjacent to the gymnasium if the two are on the same floor.

2. Limit halls to the very minimum. It costs money to enclose, heat, and clean hall space. The hall is not particularly a service unit if adequate pupil circulation within the building can be provided without it. Some halls are necessary and must be provided, but in general the space enclosed by the outer walls should be used for service units rather than for unnecessary halls. If possible, passage should be directly outdoors from the locker room. The line of traffic to the outdoors should not cross the line of traffic to the showers.

3. Avoid placing another room over the swimming pool, if possible. If this cannot be avoided, the floor of the room above should be damp-proofed.

4. Have stairs lead directly from the locker room to the gymnasium and wide enough for a line of traffic to go down while another line is coming up, provided the

gymnasium is on the floor above, as is customary. This avoids the necessity of passing through cold halls, helps keep students with street shoes off the gym floor, and saves space.

5. Provide outdoor exits and stairs, if necessary, from main gym floor. These serve particularly well when crowds use the gymnasium.

Materials and Construction

The funds available, the materials at hand, the use to which the constructed part is to be put, the attitude of the community toward types of construction and materials, and the workmen available at the time will determine quite largely the quality and type of material and construction that will contribute to each finished unit in the building. If funds are ample and the community desires to use them, there can be relatively great freedom of choice in materials and construction. However, most communities must build economically, if at all, and consequently wish to select serviceable, reasonably priced materials and put them together in a comparatively inexpensive but substantial manner. In economizing, it is best to use materials of a good standard grade; it is false economy to use cheap materials. The cost and availability of fireproofed material should be considered by those who plan to build. The various major parts of a building, including fixtures, will be considered in turn from the viewpoint of materials and construction.

The placement or arrangement of fixtures will also be discussed. In the construction of all building parts the first important step is to secure reliable contractors or workmen, and the next is to provide for inspection of the work as it is being done. There are two general types of floor to consider: (1) those for the shower, locker, and swimming pool rooms, and (2) those for the other activity rooms, standard classrooms, and offices. A hard, impervious floor is best for the first type since it is much less affected by moisture and can be more readily cleaned than wood, cork, or other less hard surfaces. Of the commonly use materials cement is the most economical and, consequently, the most generally used. Tile, however, makes an excellent surface but is too expensive to be used widely. More communities can afford to furnish it is shower rooms and around swimming pools than in locker and other auxiliary rooms.

Although wood is warmer for bare feet, it is not to be recommended since it warps and deteriorates when exposed to damp air and water. Linoleum placed over rough cement serves quite well for floors of this type. The floors should be sloped gradually to the drains, which should be large enough to prevent overflow to other rooms, especially from the shower room, which is most is most liable to overflow. The janitor's work should be made as easy and convenient as possible; hence, a floor that slopes to the drain and has no low, undrained sections for puddles is important. If it can be cared for with a hose and squeegee, a janitor should not be expected to use the more unpleasant and unsanitary mop. Occasionally the floor will need a thorough scrubbing with some strongly alkaline soap cleaner and a brush, but usually it just needs to have the dust and loose dirt washed off. The floor surface is very important. If it is too rough, it collects dirt and is very hard to clean; but if it is too smooth, the pupils have difficulty standing on it when it is wet.

A compromise must then be made between the rough and the smooth which results in a medium finish, smooth enough to permit efficient cleaning but not so slippery that it is dangerous to use when wet. Pulverized steel missed with the surface finish helps produce a satisfactory surface. Nonskid floor for shower and locker rooms, consisting of Neoprene material, are available from the Gates Manufacturing Company of Wellington, Del. Talc or other grit and a germicide may be added to the surface finish, which may be put on as a heavy paint. If apparatus fastening are to be used in the floor, they should be placed there before the floor is finished, for the sake of economy and appearance. Raised cement locker bases should be installed at the time or shortly after the floor is laid. Wood and cork are commonly used for the top flooring in offices, activity rooms, and standard classrooms. Wood is generally more serviceable and economical. Some commercial types of wood flooring serve quite well, but the most commonly used satisfactory woods are hard maple and pecan. Long, narrow strips of tongued and grooved material are recommended because they have less shrinkage and small cracks. Short lengths are not satisfactory, because there are too many cross cracks and too many chances for bits of the ends to chip off.

The flooring should be seasoned and dry when it is put in. Pine and oak are more acceptable for the office and standard classroom floors than for the activity room floors. As stated above, in constructing these floors and preparing them for use, reliable workmen and regular inspection are essential. If the floor is to be placed on the ground, damp-proofing material should be used; then a ventilated air space should be left to prevent mildew and dry rot, and the floor proper should be placed above this. The floor proper, whether next to the ground or in a story above, should consist of sleepers, rough flooring, good building paper, and then the finished floor. Once the floor are in, they should be sanded and treated with an appropriate finish. There are several good commercial once on the market. They are serviceable and stand up under cleaning and use remarkably well. Since the commercial companies are constantly improving their products and fitting them to specific need, they can provide the type of finish desired and are glad to do so with instructions concerning proper methods of application. After it is sanded, but before the finish dressing is applied, lines in different colours and widths for there or four different games should be painted on the main gym floor; the special activity rooms should have just the lines for the game involved painted on the floor. Too many lines confuse the players who try to use the activity area.

Walls—There are many qualifications and service purposes, some general and others specific, that need to be met by satisfactory walls. Generally all walls should serve as at least partial barriers to the passage of sound, moisture, light, air, heat, and foreign materials.

They should not be too expensive, but they should make a good appearance. No wall should constitute a particular hazard because of its rough or uneven surface, or because of the likelihood that it may fall down, burn, or afford a breeding place for harmful bacteria and fungus growths. Beside their general purposes, some walls need to serve specifically as rebounding surfaces for balls, others as places to attach apparatus, others as acoustical material, others as reflectors of light, and still others as particularly efficient barriers to the passage of moisture or sound. Since practically all of the outside and main partition walls are made of brick, tile, or cement, any of which are satisfactory, we shall consider particularly the wall finish or inner part of the wall. Glazed brick, hollow glazed tile, and smooth cement are all good materials. The glazed bricks are more expensive but make a better appearance. Cement makes a poor appearance. All of these materials are firm enough to serve as a rebounding surface, smooth enough to furnish no hazard, noninflammable, generally impervious, reasonably economical, and easily cleaned.

They are not good acoustical material, for echoes are easily set up between hard finished wall. Wood is a better acoustical material for large rooms, but it may constitute a fire hazard. It is too much affected by moisture to be used in the shower or locker rooms. Ordinary plaster is not generally satisfactory because it will not resist moisture or the impact of balls and players; however, it may be used in offices, standard classrooms, and above the 12-foot to 15-foot levels in the main gym rooms. Hard finishing plaster is used for handball courts and other surfaces where an exact bounce is necessary. Granted the necessary materials, workmen, and inspection service which should insure substantial walls, there are several additional items that should be considered.

1. If the walls extend below the surface of the ground, all outside walls should be damp-proofed from the bottom to a foot above the surface of the ground.

2. A dead air space between the inner and outside walls will provide insulation against sound, cold, and heat.

3. The inner wall surface should be smooth, especially where activity groups are to come in contact with it, to reduce the number of abrasions.

4. A rough collects dirt.

5. Light coloured walls reflect light better and provide a more cheerful atmosphere.

6. The shower room walls might well be white.

7. Fastening for equipment and apparatus should be placed in the wall before the finish surface is put on.

8. Angle irons screwed to the floor where the floor meets the wall will round the corner and facilitate cleaning.

9. If the wall is to be used for a rebounding surface, it should be free from windows, radiators, and pipes to a height of 12 feet or more.

10. If the plumbing is not already in, openings of proper size should be left in all walls through which pipes are to pass.

In regions infested with termites special protection is required for the wood parts of walls and other units of construction. This can be done by preventing the exposure of underpinning and sills to dampness, by avoiding ground connections to weed parts, and by impregnating the wood with chemicals toxic to termites.

Roof and Ceiling—Flaws in the roof are usually very expensive, for they are often them may damage or destroy valuable equipment or construction within the building. Consequently, it is imperative that an adequate roof be placed over the physical education building. In constructing smaller buildings, a satisfactory roof is not much of a problem, probably because of the greater slope of the roof and relatively of the commercial types of roofing prove satisfactory. Wood shingles present more of a fire hazard than other materials, and tile is more expensive. Securing an adequate roof for large physical education buildings is a greater problem. Large, flat surfaces, which allow water to remain longer and require several roofing units to be fitted together, thus increasing danger from storms during construction, should be avoided. Materials are important, of course, but any small error in putting them together is apt to cause a leak. For this reason it is of prime importance that the contract be let to an extremely reliable firm, on that can be depended upon to provide a roof without leaks that will last a reasonable length of time.

The firm selected should be granted the privilege of selecting materials according to the specifications set up. More freedom of choice should be given the contractor in the case of the roof because small defects are so important; exact workmanship in this case is relatively much more important than in most other phases of construction, where fair workmanship and good materials will often suffice. Ceiling materials vary considerably according to the room. For offices, standard classrooms, and high gymnasium rooms plaster is satisfactory; for shower, locker, and auxiliary rooms cement, glazed brick, or tile are recommended. If apparatus is to be fastened to the ceiling, all necessary clamps and fasteners should be installed before the ceiling is finished. A light ceiling has the same general lighting advantages as light walls.

Windows—In addition to serving as a barrier against the elements, windows have the double function of providing for ventilation and admitting natural light. Either of these functions may be replaced by artificial or mechanical means, but at a considerably greater cost. Hence the window space should be sufficiently large and properly arranged to care for these two function under normal daytime conditions. The lighting function must be supplemented by artificial lights on dark days and at night, but in most cases the ventilating function can be cared and at night, but in most cases the ventilating function can be cared for adequately by means of windows. Mechanical ventilation has its supporters, but studies of natural versus mechanical ventilation do not present any more conclusive evidence in favour of the mechanical type than in favour of the natural type. Expert opinion on this is also divided. In case of doubt it is probably a more advisable procedure to select the more economical, less complicated type of ventilation. In certain cases mechanical ventilation is necessary, particularly in locker rooms and in places where just a few suction fans will suffice for these sections of a large building.

When questions arise about the advisability of providing air conditioning, they should be answered only after checking with specialists. The louvres type of window serves very well in ventilating, with a minimum of drafts and provides protection from rain, sleet, and snow. The single pivot section, fastened in the centre and swinging out at the bottom and in at the top tends to break air currents and act as a shelter against the elements, while admitting air at top and bottom. A double pivot section, one above the other, would serve both purposes better and be easier to screen, because it would not project so far out, or in, from the plane of the window, however, it would cost more and provide more cracks to admit cold air in the winter or a droving rain in the summer. Some authorities recommend central electrical control of windows for ventilation purposes. This is hardly advisable, for those the room in question are in a much better position to know the ventilation requirements than is someone in the director's office.

The window panes should not be too large, for many are broken and the replacement cost is decidedly less for small ones. Translucent glass should be used for locker and shower room windows and in the gymnasium or basketball court windows on the west if there are any. It is sometimes advisable to have the same type in the windows on the west half of the south side since the floor is practically always in use during late afternoon. If the floor is to be used in early morning, east windows may need to have translucent glass, too. Windows in activity rooms where balls are used should be screened, except when they are high enough to be relatively free from the danger of being hit. Sliding screens of number eight wire are recommended. In efficiency of illumination, as in efficiency of ventilation, the placement of the windows is as important as the total window area, because distance from the source of light is an important factor. Light intensity is measured in terms of foot candles.

A foot candle is the amount of light thrown by one international candle upon a perpendicular surface at a distance of one foot. This same unit of light at a distance of several feet is greatly reduced, for candlepower decreases inversely as the square of the distance. Thus 64-foot candles become 16-foot candles at two feet, one-foot candle at eight feet, one-fourth foot candle at 16 feet, and only one sixty-fourth-foot candle at 64 feet-a little more than the distance across a fair sized gym. It is evident that one half the light at one half the distance is twice as intense as twice the light at twice the distance. Consequently, one half the window area distributed on opposite side of the floor will serve much better from the point of view of intensity of light where needed than will twice the window area on just one side. According to generally accepted standards of illumination, from 15-20 foot candles of light are sufficient for activity in which exact seeing is not important.

This is the type presented in activity classes, except when small, fast-moving balls, such as tennis balls, are used. Direct sunlight measures about 10,000 foot candles; on average cloudy days this is reduced to from 1,000 to 2,000 foot candles. Hence, it is very difficult to determine the exact amount of window space needed. In accord with the above facts the ratio of one fourth to one fifth of the total floor area in window area is satisfactory, provided the windows are on opposite sides of the gymnasium, provided the windows are on opposite sides of the gymnasium. However this may interfere with vision somewhat because of cross lighting. For smaller rooms the ratio of one fourth to one fifth is adequate. Skylights are not to be recommended very highly because of the difficulties involved in making them function properly. They often condense moisture, which may drop on the floor, or they may cause drafts when open, fail to keep out rain, and permit the sun to shine directly on certain parts of the floor, all of which may interfere with activities.

Door—Wood, glass, reinforcing wire, copper, brass,

and iron or steel are commonly combined to make satisfactory doors for any part of the physical education building. The specific purpose to be served will dictate the proper combination of the above materials. The funds available and the use and treatment the door can be expected to withstand should influence its selection. If light must enter through the door or vision is to be unobstructed, a section of glass is necessary; translucent glass is desirable if only light is to enter. If the door is to be subjected to alternate wetting and drying, as in the shower room, a covering of copper will reduce expansion and contraction. However, the copper may add more to the cost than funds will permit.

If the door is to receive rough usage, rugged construction, brass kick plates, non-shatter glass, and protective bars over the glass are desirable features. If the door is to span a large space, strong but comparatively light construction is essential. Other significant points to consider is selecting and installing satisfactory doors are these:

1. Door stops should be provided to keep doors from being "banged" to pieces.

2. Doors should open out from rather than into, main gym or activity rooms, even though a little vestibule is necessary at the head of a stairs.

3. All exit doors should open outward and be equipped with panic bolts, so that crowds may not be trapped by a locker or blocked door.

4. Doors should be fastened to expansion blots rather than wooden plugs driven into the wall since the wood is apt to work loose.

5. Large doors should be provided to gym room for use by visitors or spectators and for use in moving apparatus and materials in and out.

6. Doors should be placed in the most convenient locations to facilitate circulation of traffic within the building.

7. Folding doors should be used to separate the gymnasium into halves, if it is planned to use it for two classes at a time.

8. Strong, efficient lock should be provided for doors that need to be kept closed.

Artificial lighting—When natural light is available it should be used; but when it is not, artificial lighting becomes necessary. The intensity of light in any part of the room can be regulated by regulating the intensity of the source and by placing light bulbs and reflectors correctly. Semidirect light causes less glare and eyestrain but is a little more expensive than direct light. Fluorescent lighting is advocated by some but attacked by others. Many new buildings now include fluorescent lighting, although its superiority over the filament type of lighting is by no means universally proven. Satisfactory intensity for general physical education activity is stated above as from 15-20 foot candles; for more exact vision greater intensity is desirable. The director should consider the following points when having lighting fixtures installed.

1. In activity rooms recess lights or enclose in a protecting wire basket.

2. Provide a switches in convenient places where lights can be seen from them.

3. Be sure they are installed before the walls and ceilings are finished.

4. Leave as few wires and encasing pipes exposed as possible.

5. Provide adequate and convenient light plugs to meet needs of special occasions.

6. Place light switches in convenient places where lights can be seen from them.

7. Fasten protecting baskets to wall or ceiling rather than to light fixtures.

8. Place light so that there is a minimum of glare from them.

9. Avoid the use of key switches as much as possible.

Plumbing—In selecting plumbing equipment it is wise to purchase good standard materials from a reliable dealer. Durability, strength, simplicity of design, an good finish are the marks of satisfactory equipment.

All pipes for water, heat, gas, or other purposes and all sewage and drain pipes should be laid before the wall and the foundation are built. Care should be taken to mend the damp-proofing in the event that pipes are laid after the walls are in Toilets, showers, lavatories, cuspidors, and drinking fountains should be placed conveniently, of course, but in such position that a minimum of approach and disposal pipes are necessary. This cannot be arranges in all cases, but it can in many. Girls' showers, for instance, might as well be on the opposite side of the walls from boys' showers as in some other corner of the room or section of the building. Fewer pipes need be used, too, if the unit on the floor above is directly above the unit on the floor below. Hot and cold water pipes should be far enough apart so that the cold water remains cold, and the danger of accident is reduced if pipes are enclosed in the walls. Those factors sufficiently outweight the increased cost of installation and the greater difficulty of getting at pipes when something goes wrong, so that enclosing in the walls in recommended if provision is made for access when necessary. Specific suggestions concerning each of the following service units are presented under the unit concerned.

1. Lavatories. The planners should:

(a) provide facets that automatically close slowly if left ope.

(b) provide lavatories near toilet room.

(c) provide white porcelain finish rather than coloured finish.

(d) Provide paper towels and liquid soap in connection with the lavatories.

2. Radiators and heating. The planner should:

(a) Insulate heat pipes to conserve heat, to prevent burns, and to prevent overheating of some rooms or halls.

(b) Distribute radiators enough to provide a comparatively even temperature throughout the room.

(c) Provide sufficient radiation to furnish adequate heat on cold days-about 60⁰ F. for the activity rooms, about 70⁰ F. for the locker rooms, and about 80⁰ F. for the shower and swimming pool rooms.

(d) Recess radiators in walls or place them above them above the heights of pupils. If recessed, a few protecting bars or grates should be used. It is probably best to suspend them from the ceiling in locker rooms.

(e) Provide proportionately fewer heat units to heat large rooms than to heat small ones, for as rooms get larger the volume increases more rapidly than the area of exposed outer surface through which heat passes off. A one-inch cube has a height of one inch, a volume of one cubic inch, and a surface of six square inches; a two-inch cube has a height of two, a volume of eight, and a surface of 24 inches; and a three-inch cube has a height of three, a volume of 27, and a surface of 54 inches. In the above the ratio between volume and surface decreases from one to six, to one to three, to one to tow.

3. Showers. The planners should:

(a) Provide shower heads with removable faces so that they can be cleaned easily.

(b) Furnish soap and provide towel hooks in a convenient place for the bathers.

(c) Provide sufficient showers to care for peak load. Allow about 18 square feet for each shower, with one shower for five boys and one shower for four girls. If girls are to have individual showers and dressing booths, one shower can serve only two conveniently.

(d) Arrange showers so that water flowing from one does not interfere with the use of another shower.

(e) Provide large drain pipe from showers so that there will be no danger of overflow to other rooms.

(f) Have shower heads higher than the heads of the people who are to use them, but set them to discharge diagonally downward so that those who use them may avoid getting their heads wet if they choose.

(g) Provide for individual control of showers. Although central control is advocated as an economy measure, individual control under supervision is not particularly expensive and is much more satisfactory to the bathers. Younger children may need to be taught how to take showers, and that can be done at school with a little effort.

4. Drinking fountains. The planners should:

(a) Provide for foot release.

(b) Select a type that is not apt to squirt water out on floor.

(c) Place one just outside main activity room and another in locker room. Drinking of water should be encouraged by providing a convenient supply; consequently, additional fountains may be necessary.

(d) Select a type that throws water toward one side rather than straight up.

(e) Select a type that is not apt to squirt water out on floor.

5. Toilets. The planners should:

(a) Provide foot release for flushing. It is much more sanitary than a hand release.

(b) Regulate urinal height to fit the convenience of the boys who are to use it.

(c) Provide enough to care for peak load class; about one urinal for 25 boys and one stool for 15 girls; about one stool for 30 boys.

(d) Provide the type that flushes readily with a small

amount of water.

6. Lockers and Baskets. The planners should:

(a) Arrange lockers around the walls in small rooms.

(b) Build cement bases for the lockers.

(c) Provide ventilation for metal locker used to store equipment. They should be ventilated by sucking warm, dry air through them and out of doors.

(d) Provide aisles about five feet wide when lockers are placed in rows.

(e) Arrange lockers so that light from the windows falls between the rows.

(f) Provide two or three small locker rooms rather than one large room. One room can be cooler for those who like to dress in a cooler room. One small room can then be used for the visiting team's locker room when visitors come to compete. This is an essential courtesy that should be extended to visitors; for they are guests of the institution and should be given the guest room, with the privacy it affords when they desire it.

7. Cuspidors. The planners should:

(a) Provide for removal or swinging back of bars for cleaning.

(b) Provide a type that will flush easily with a little water.

(c) Provide foot-flush type.

(d) Select a different coloured finish from that of the drinking fountain.

(e) Place at least one in main gym room, recessed in

wall with bars to keep balls out of it. This is essential since some players must expectorate during activity periods, and if no proper place is provided the floor or wall will have to suffice.

Locker Unit—Lockers and baskets vary greatly in the matter of sizes, materials used in construction, and methods of handing. The wire type allows clothes to dry much better than the metal louvre type but are easier to break into and admit more dust and water. Larger, full-length lockers are more convenient and adequate than the small 12 × 12 × 36 inch type but also more expensive.

The problem, then, is to provide that combination of lockers and baskets that most adequately meets the needs of the various groups concerned without entailing too great expense. It is generally agreed that the varsity athletes should have individual lockers placed in the varsity locker room. Full-length lockers are recommended, but if funds will not permit them, half-length lockers can be made to do. Each locker should have a good strong lock on it. The master-key-combination type is recommended. The inside of the floor should be painted white to improve visibility. Some school provide half-length lockers for all students who use the locker rooms, and a few provide full-length lockers for all.

This is very convenient but too expensive to be recommended for general use. Some combination of basket and locker systems is much better. There are three reasonably good systems: two with attendants on duty during class time, and one without. In all three systems there are enough full-length lockers provided to care for the peak load. This includes class members, going and combing, recreational activity people, and intramural competitors. These lockers might be distributed in two or three smaller locker rooms or, in the event locked basket compartments are used, around the walls of the room which contains the baskets. In one of the systems requiring an attendant, two rows of baskets are situated back to back. Each basket is locked in its compartment with a master-key-combination lock.

The student gets his basket and changes his clothing, putting his street clothes in an adjacent full-length locker provided for that purpose and locking it with the padlock which was on his basket compartment. An equipment exchange window is maintained at which the student can get clean clothes at the end of his exercise period. In the other system requiring an attendant, as in the one above, each person using the locker room has basket with his assigned number on it. The baskets are placed on shelves in the basket room; those for each class in the same section of the basket room. When a student desires his basket, he calls out his number and the attendant slides the basket along a chute to him. The wire basket, about 15 × 10 × 20 inches, contains his gym clothes, a clean towel, and the padlock for the locker in which he is to keep his street clothes. He selects his locker and uses it. When he has taken his shower and is ready to leave, he slides his basket into the chute.

The attendant puts in a clean towel and places the basket back on the rack in the stall containing its number. The third basket-locker system recommended here does not require an attendant on duty during the time baskets are used. The locker arrangement is the same as above, but the basket arrangement differs. The same type of baskets, with numbers on them and corresponding numbers on their individual compartments, is recommended; but these baskets are placed around the outside of a series of hollow oblong cages. The cages project outward somewhat like the spoken from a hub but more like the fingers of four hands crossed at the wrists. In the central, or wrist, area is the equipment room. Above the total basket setup is heavy wire fencing to provide ventilation and safety for equipment. Each cage is about 20 to 30 feet in length, 8 feet in width, and 6 feet in height, exclusive of the wire fencing above it. Heavy wire compartments around the outer part of the cage are arranged in five tiers to contain students' baskets.

The passageway down the centre of the hollow cage is wide enough to permit servicing the individual baskets from two large baskets on rollers, one for used clothes and one for clean clothes. The student's basket is constructed low enough in the back, toward the inside of the cage, to permit the attendant to exchange towels and clothing issued by the department and to check equipment. A tray is provided in the upper part of the back of the student's basket to contain the clothing which is to be exchanged. Two bars extend across the basket on which to put damp clothing so that it will dry better. A metal door on the front of the compartment, toward the outside, is provided with a good master-key-combination padlock. This lock can also be used on the locker when the student leaves his street clothes there. The student may take his basket from its compartment when he needs it and return it when he is through with it. This system is economical, convenient, and sanitary.

The following locker room accessories are desirable.

1. A bulletin board near the entrance to locker room

or rooms.

2. Benches for all lockers. Long benches fastened to the floor by steel posts serve very well.

3. Hair dryers for the girls' locker room.

4. Mirrors for both girls and boys. One in each small locker room, and at least one at each end of the large locker room, if there is a large locker room.

5. Dressing booths for girls. It is satisfactory to provide booths for more girls are accepting the type of dressing facilities and showers used by boys.

Apparatus

Apparatus should be selected on the basis of its prospective usefulness in furthering a modern physical education program rather than because of traditional support of the activity for which it will be used. Traditional support does not condemn it, but in itself is not sufficient to determine the selection of apparatus. Rugged, simple, standard pieces should be chosen. Even though the original cost may be greater, the difference will be compensated for in reduced repair bills. Since shipping costs for heavy pieces are relatively high, it may be more economical to purchase from some dealer close at hand. Mobile pieces that can be fastened to floor or wall catches or thrown of rollers by means of a lever are recommended.

When the apparatus has been used, it can then be swung back against the wall, raised to the ceiling, or rolled off to the apparatus room, leaving the main floor available for other activities. Mats and smaller pieces that require no fastening should be stored out of the way on a platform on wheels and in boxes on wheels.

Swimming Unit

The significance of swimming as an activity for elementary and high school students during the regular school year has probably been overemphasized by physical education people. Swimming, however, if it can be financed, is an excellent activity when conducted in the most favourable surroundings. Many of the essential elements of optimum surroundings are present in the outdoor pool during the warm months of the year. From the viewpoint of an adequate, economical physical education setup in high schools in the northern states, it is sound procedure to dispense with inside pools and swimming during the months when clods are most prevalent and costs of heating water and providing swimming facilities are highest, except in some of the larger cities. The money for the school swimming program can be more economically spent by providing swimming facilities under adequate instruction and supervision in the warm months when students care most about swimming.

This will do away with the ever present group of youngsters who have excuses, legitimate and otherwise, for staying out of the water, and it will provide a valuable supervised recreational period during the summer. However, many physical educators and the communities which they represent are not yet ready to break with tradition and provide activities, in the absence of precedent, at the time they serve their purpose best. Since this is true, funds that could provide more adequate facilities for other activities during the school year will continue to be used to provide inside swimming units in the larger communities.

Colleges and universities have additional needs for

inside pools for teacher-training purposes and varsity competition. Then, too, college students are apt to be away from school during the summer, when students in the pre-college ages can be expected to get their training in swimming in the local pool. Consequently, the following suggestions are presented concerning swimming pools.

1. For one pool, the depth should range from 3 feet at shallow end to 11 feet at deepest point, and the slopes should be gradual until the approach to the deep end, where the slope should be increased. For colleges the depth at shallow end might well be 4 feet.

2. A space of 6 to 8 feet with nonslip surface and free from obstacles, should be provided all around the pool.

3. Lanes, 7 feet apart, should be marked or built in, using dark-coloured tile, if pool is to be used for competitive purposes.

4. The pool should not be placed in a dark hole in the basement. Instead, ample light and clearance should be provided above the pool. It is well to place the pool on the south side of building to get more sunlight.

5. A separate door should be provided for spectators to use, and all spectators in street clothes should be excluded from the area surrounding pool.

6. It is a good plan to secure the services of a contractor who has built several successful pools.

7. Deep scum gutters should be provided to drain away sputum, materials washed in from the water surface, and materials washed in from around the pools, and to serve as hand hold for swimmers.

8. Surface finishing materials for floor and walls of pool should be light coloured glazed brick or tile.

9. A pool 75 feet long by 35 feet wide is adequate for most school purposes, although one 42 feet wide is more desirable. Two smaller pools, one deep and the other shallow, are better for school purposes than is one large pool.

10. If possible a chlorinating, or brominating, and filtering system should be provided to destroy harmful bacteria, and a vacuum cleaner to remove dirt. Additional sanitation suggestions include.

(a) The use of alum to help coagulate bacteria.

(b) A "differential bacteria count" of samples of pool water, in which the number of bacteria of each type are counted.

(c) Treatment of water so that it does not have to be changed frequently.

(d) A heat unit which introduces steam into the recirculating system.

(e) The use of chlorine or bromine; both economical, satisfactory chemicals, to keep down harmful bacteria count. Bromine probably irritates less.

(f) The use one ppm. of copper sulphate to destroy algae effectively.

(g) A test to determine chlorine content. The orthotolidine test is a simple one. Liquid in glass tubes, graded according to amount of red colouring matter, is used. Another liquid is provided, with instructions as to amount to add to samples of water of specified volume from the pool. The samples of water are then compared with the standard coloured tubes. Chlorine content is indicated by amount of red colouring in water. Each tube is labelled with the ppm. of chlorine that a sample of treated water of the same colour contains. A content of 0.2 ppm. to 0.5 ppm. is considered satisfactory. Bacteria content is controlled by chlorine content. Most water laboratories can furnish more detailed information on this point.

(f) A bacteria count. This will not give the number of harmful bacteria, but the total number of all the bacteria present reflects the probable number of harmful bacteria.

11. When the pool does not have a chlorinating or recirculating system, it is advisable to use hypochlorite drawn through the pool in a bag or porous bucket to destroy harmful bacteria. The water should be changed often enough to keep the pool clean. Swimmers should be kept out of the pool for several hours after it is treated by the above method, for certain parts of it will contain concentrated chlorine.

12. In operating the pool the following practices should be observed:

(a) Discourage the practice of dangerous stunts in and around the pool.

(b) Require simple cotton or woollen suits for girls but let boys swim without suits, except for mixed groups.

(c) Use a suction cleaner to clean dirt off bottom and sides of the pool.

(d) Test daily for temperature and chlorine content of water.

(e) Provide a competent lifeguard at all times when

the pool is in use.

(f) Require all who use the pool to have a medical examination, to be free from sores, and to bathe with soap before entering pool.

Outdoor Activity Areas

The following general points should be kept in mind in planning outdoor physical education activity areas:

1. The lighting should be planned to avoid glare and dark spots, place wires underground, and provide a good general appearance.

2. Sections of the general area should be set aside for the less rugged competitors.

3. A few drinking fountains should be placed in protected spots near activity areas. These should be provided with a foot release.

4. Those parts that must be protected or fenced should be located along the sides or ends of the general area.

5. If possible a conveniently located area should be selected.

6. Walks should not interfere with play areas but should be laid, in so far as possible, to fit the natural lines of traffic. This means rounded corners and following traffic short cuts.

7. Provision should be made for storing equipment and supplies near the areas where they will be used.

8. Activity area should be consulted concerning the various problems that arise in connection with lighting, landscaping, fencing, drainage, and the construction

of specific areas.

9. Fields, such as football fields, to which the public must have convenient access, should be placed to one side, or better still, in a convenient corner of the general play area.

10. Most play areas should be fenced. A suitable fence for many locations consists of 11-gauge woven wire 10 feet high. This will protect property, provide privacy, reduce supervising problems, and keep balls and other play materials from rolling, or being carried into the street.

11. Surfacing materials should be selected to fit the budget, the needs for the activities, and the welfare of the students.

12. Correct planning leaves no small plates of unusable size in the corners or along the sides of the area. It is a good plan to leave all unscheduled or unmarked space together, rather than in small plates here and there, where they cannot be used as a general play area.

13. Provision should be made for adequate surface and subsurface drainage.

14. Some area other than the streets should be provided for parking space in the vicinity. An acre of ground will accommodate about 150 cars.

15. Specific play areas should be so placed that participants will be handicapped as little as possible by the sun, the wind, and contours of the ground.

16. Specialists should be consulted concerning the various problems that arise in connection with lighting,

landscaping, fencing, drainage, and the construction of specific areas.

17. Provisions should be made for multiple use of fields during different parts of the day, or night, and during different seasons.

Baseball Fields

A considerable problem arises in orienting baseball diamonds so that both the players and the spectators will be handicapped as little as possible. For professional games the spectators often receive more consideration than they do for school contests. The school diamonds should be laid out to favour the players, for they are of prime importance and often they play without spectators. For schools it is satisfactory to have the base line from home to first base run directly west. This will reduce considerably interference with vision by the afternoon sun. Adequate back stops should be provided to reduce lost balls and ball chasing in general and to protect spectators. The distance from home plate and the size of the back stop will depend upon space and materials available. The construction and care of the diamond is important.

The area should be approximately level, with adequate provision for drainage. The pitcher's plate may be elevated on a gradually sloping mound not higher than 18 inches above the grass should be kept mowed in both the infield and outfield. If the sod is removed from the base paths and other sections of the infield, those areas need care before each game. If water is available, they are customarily wet down, raked, and rolled, after which, first and third base lines are extended, and the boxes at home plate are marked with line. Permanent markers on the foul lines in deep right and left field are valuable aids in judging fair and foul balls.

Football Fields

The football field should be laid out and constructed in such a manner that it will be the most adequate playing area possible. In order that the team defending the least favoured goal may be handicapped as little as possible by the sun and the wind the layout must be considered carefully. Since the prevailing winds in most sections of the country blow from the west, and since the sun shines from the west in the late fall afternoon it is often best to lay out the field north and south if possible. Other factors may make this undesirable but, in general, it is well to keep this in mind. The field and adjacent territory should be well drained.

This is especially important if it is located on low ground. Coarse gravel a couple feet under the surface soil, which is composed of 8-12 inches to one foot of loam, with well-placed tile will aid materially in quick drainage. Most fields are already constructed without a gravel base and cannot be rebuilt. Tile alone may help considerably in such cases.

The field should be about 8 inches higher in the centre than at the sideline and should slope gradually and evenly to the sides of the playing area to allow water to drain off quickly rather than stand in pools any place on the field.

The surface soil should be of the type that will maintain a good growth of grass. Fertilizer and lime may need to be added at times. Water pipes so laid that there are adequate outlets for hose connections will simplify greatly the problem of watering in those regions where summer drought causes a problem. The outlets must be far enough under the surface and well enough enclosed that there will be no danger of injury to players from them.

Tennis Courts

Perhaps the most satisfactory layout position for tennis courts would be from northwest to southeast. However, courts as a rule are not placed at an angle, so that north and south position is most common.

There are many regions in the United States, especially in the northern part, where hard surface courts are almost essential if tennis is to be played in the spring of the year. This is true to a limited extent in the other sections of the country.

Grass courts for schools will not stand up under the regular play which they will get during the tennis season. Clay or dirt courts are not only unfit for play after a rain but remain unfit until they are rolled and marked. In many schools it is difficult to free some one of the building and grounds staff just when the courts need to be serviced. That means additional unused time.

Cement is one of the most satisfactory surfacing materials. The cost is high, but if properly laid, a cement court will last a long time. Proper laying includes good drainage around the edge and under the court, coarse gravel and rock base to a depth of 12-18 inches, then coarse cement, and finally a finish surface of fine cement. The surface must not be too smooth, or players will experience difficulty in keeping their footing. Asphalt is much more economical than cement but need repair and replacement in a comparatively short time.

There are a number of specific tennis court surface preparations that are also good. Manufacturers will gladly provide information and assistance in building courts using their prepared surfacing materials. Backstops, about 21 feet from the base line and 12 feet high are recommended. A group of courts might well be enclosed by a 12-foot fence.

Putting Green Grass

Green greens are to be preferred to other greens but require expert care and considerable cost for upkeep. If a green is to have heavy use, as it might well have as an approaching and putting green at school, some surface that will stand more abuse at a lower cost is better. Coarse sand with enough oil to keep it from drying out and blowing away may serve very well. A smoothing device to prepare two strips at right angles from one side of the green to the other, crossing at the hole, will enable students to smooth off a putting strip as they wish to use it. Cotton seed greens require comparatively little upkeep and provide a fair putting surface.

Track

A convenient arrangement for most schools that have booth track and football is that of placing the track around the football fields. This is economical of space and places of the performers in both sports in positions where they can be observed from the same bleachers.

3

The Position of Physical Education in Education

In establishing the position of physical education in the pattern of general education it is important to present in brief the role of physical education in the past, and to indicate in what way the purposes of physical education are in accord with, or contribute to, the goals of education. This will be done in the light of the present day philosophy of physical education as it is reflected in modern courses of study, in the significant writings in the field, and in the need of physical education in our society.

Historical Background

From a brief review of the evidence of the past well shall see that the amount and type of physical education practised by a people reflects its philosophy and frequently reveals the dominant purpose of the state. Some people of the past who believed in subjugating the body as a means of elevating the soul discouraged enjoyable physical activity and, as a result, did very little toward developing a physical education program.

However, the Egyptians, Babylonians, and Hebrews, with a higher regard for the physical, encouraged and engaged in numerous sports and, consequently, developed more extensive physical education program. Persia, under Cyrus, a dominant leader, revolted from Media about 558 b.c Cyrus had a philosophy of conquest and a major purpose that physical education could serve. He needed soldiers who could fight well and who could take care of themselves on the march. Consequently, he took young boys at about the age of six and trained them in discipline, running, jumping, javelin throwing, mounting, raiding, and other skills that would build more efficient fighting men. To test and develop his troops, Cyrus held long hunts which were severe ordeals. Extended marches, little food, and meagre protection from the elements characterized this phase of training.

The education of boys stressed primarily the physical and moral aspects-those moral aspects that would make for better fighters. Since the girls were not needed as soldiers, their education was neglected. About two centuries later, a philosophy of ease coupled with corrupt practices led to a neglect of rigorous training and to disregard for physical efficiency. This undermined the strength of Persia and, as a result, Alexander conquered her with ease. The Spartans, somewhat after the time of Cyrus, had a philosophy and purpose similar to that of the Persians and developed the same type of physical education.

The boys were take by the state at about the age of seven housed in barracks, and trained in those attitudes and forms of physical activity that made for stoic, rugged soldiers. Jumping, running, wrestling, throwing weights, and mimic dances of warfare were among the important physical activities. To provide more surely for strong fighting men, the weak and poorly formed babies were exposed to die. Spartan girls were trained physically so that they would become better mothers. Athens had military needs comparable to those of Sparta and Persia, but had a somewhat different philosophy. Learning, beauty, and grace loomed larger in the picture of Athenian life; less rigor and more freedom was the standard for men.

The physical education of women was given very little consideration. The physical activities were practically the same as those of Sparta, but additional aspects of performance were stressed. Beauty, grace, and sportsmanship were added to speed, courage, strength, and skill. This philosophy spread and made, itself felt during Greek control of the Panhellenic games, the most noted of which were the Olympic games. During the growth and rise of Rome as a would power hard work and physical exercise that prepared the young for war were dictated by a philosophy of conquest. At the crest of its power, and especially during its decline, Rome was aflame with a desire to see blood.

The physical activities of its great arenas reflected this desire. Dangerous chariot races, gladiatorial contests, beast baiting, miniature battles, extremely rough fighting, and brutal ball games marked this epoch of Roman Life. The Dark Ages, with the revival of asceticism, produced a general lack of interest in physical activity. Centuries later Jahan, of Germany, used physical activity and its accompanying attitudes to build to ward the great German goal of defeating France. Ling, of Sweden, saw in formal physical drill a means of improving the efficiency of the Swedish army.

This fear of neighbours and the desire for conquest have been responsible for certain types of physical education down through the ages. Even England, with her island seclusion and the resulting protection which permitted more athletic games and less mass drill, outlawed golf at one time because it interfered with archery practice. The Puritans and other early settlers in America, who had a great deal of work to do, frowned upon those types of play that did not consist of some work form. Wood-chopping contests, corn-husking contests, and rifle matches were popular. More recently, however, increased leisure, greater freedom of thought, and a philosophy of success have led to a variety of vigorous, competitive games in the United States not modelled after work forms.

The depression, with its enforced leisure for millions, stimulated recreational centre activities. The military draft figures for World War I disclosed numerous physical defects, and as a result many states enacted compulsory physical education laws.

Although the intention was good, there is not much that additional physical education laws and activity courses can do to reduce defects of the type that cause draft rejection. Draft figures from World War II supports this point. We see, then, that the philosophy of a people, which is always formulated in part by its needs, determines both the form and the amount of its physical activity. Hence, it is important that we consider the organization and administration of those forms of physical activity that are in harmony with our present philosophy, for those are the forms with which we shall have to deal. Certain activities, formerly discouraged, are now important units in our physical education programs; others, once of major significance, are now of only minor concern. We must follow our educational philosophy, which is influenced considerably in its application by public opinion.

With What Are Organization and Administration Concerned?

Sound organization and administration are concerned with setting up or planning the total purposes and activities of the department or unit and carrying these out to the end that all important aspects involved are accomplished. Organization includes setting up the over-all pattern or plan, whereas administration deals with putting it into operation and keeping it functioning. In the physical education department the major phases with which organization and administration deal are over-all policies, facilities and equipment, human relations, budgeting and finance, staff selection, programs of physical and academic activities, details of class and team management, publicity, student problems, and aims and objective.

It is desirable that the student at this stage realize that a course in organization and administration is a summary type of course in organization and administration is a summary type of course which touches upon and re-emphasizes many phases of the program which have gone before and which ties together the entire offering in the field of physical education to give an overview of the whole departmental offering. In the whole process should be developed the viewpoint that the administrator who would accomplish his purposes best must act wisely, be friendly, strive to keep associates happy, make decisions, be reliable and honest, have a good general understanding of the entire unit involved, and be willing to accept responsibility.

The Present Outlook

These are some of the outstanding elements in our philosophy that point to the wisdom of dealing with the organization and administration of certain phases of physical education, along with some of the topics they indicate as worthy of consideration:

1. Realization of the fact that physical education should be educational.—Relation of Physical education to general education.

2. More concern about thorough establishment of bases upon which to operate a program.—(a) Aims and objectives of physical education and (b) administrative policies and activities.

3. Concentration upon developing better content and methods in physical activity classes.—(a) The physical education service program and (b) physical education class details.

4. Emphasis on more adequate preparation and higher certification standards for faculty members.—Physical education staff.

5. Increased interest in the teaching of health.—Health education.

6. Greater national and local emphasis on providing more and better school facilities.—Physical education plant.

7. A marked interest in interschool athletics.—

Interschool athletics.

8. More enthusiasm for athletics for all.—Intramural athletics.

9. A conviction that we must learn to do by doing, to lead by leading.—Student leadership.

10. Tendency to check more carefully on school expenditures.—Budget making and finance.

11. Greater concern about securing and maintaining safe, well constructed, nice-appearing equipment.—Purchase and care of equipment.

12. Recognition of the value of maintaining friendly relations with the public.—Public relations in physical education.

13. Greater concern about the legal responsibilities involved in conducting a physical education program.—Legal liability for injuries.

14. More emphasis on efficient office procedure.—Office management.

15. Increased interest in national and local organization and societies.—Physical education organization.

16. Strong emphasis on research and evaluation of public performance.—Tests and measurements in physical education.

Major Topics to Be Considered

A survey of the courses dealing with organization and administration of physical, and related subjects, in a number of the leading schools of physical education shows that the above topics are given marked consideration in many of them. Current writings in the field also emphasize the importance of the above topics in the area of organization and administration of physical education. Consequently, in the remainder of this book the following major topics will be considered in turn:

- Relationship of physical education to general education
- Aims and objectives of physical education
- Administrative policies and activities
- The physical education service program
- The physical education staff.
- School health education
- The physical education plant
- Interschool athletics
- Intramural athletics
- Student leaders in physical education
- Budget making and finance
- Purchase and care of equipment
- Public relations in physical education
- Legal liability for injury
- Office management
- Physical education organizations
- Tests and measurements in physical education

Physical Education an Integral Part of Education

Physical education is that part of education which

proceeds by means of, or predominantly through, physical activity; it is not some separate, partially related field. This significant means of education furnishes one angle of approach in educating the entire individual, who is composed of many component, interrelated functional units, rather than of several distinctly compartmentalized faculties. The physical, mental, and social aspects must all be considered together. Physical education, when well taught, can contribute more to the goals of general education than can any other school subject; not more to each goal than any other subject but more to all goals than any other school subject.

This is made possible, in part, by the fact that participation in physical education is very largely on the level at which the youngsters live. They grant their coaches and teachers great authority; the instructors in physical education have less need to demand it than do most other teachers. Opportunity for excellent achievement knocks continually at the door of the physical educator, making physical education one of the most keen-edged tools in the educational kit. With it he may sculpture beautiful figures or hack to pieces and mutilate the already partially shaped raw material that comes to him. In discussing contributions, we assume that a reasonably skilled teacher is in charge, for even the most perfect system or machine will not function well without competent direction.

The Goals of Education

The seven objectives presented in Cardinal Principles of Secondary Education are generally accepted as adequate goals of education. They are health, command of the fundamental processes, worthy home membership, vocation, citizenship, worthy use of leisure, and ethical character. A committee of leading educators appointed by the national Education Association in 1913 spent three years preparing this bulletin. Many years have passed since the bulletin appeared, and still the basic ideas of these objectives have not been replaced by others for the great mass of educators.

However, some have altered them a little here or there to balance their own personal equation. Certain writers have overemphasized particular cases; sporadic attacks have been launched from time to time by others; and many have expressed the same ideas in different terms; but these seven objectives still stand as adequate and acceptable goals of American education. It is worth noting in this connection that the Educational Policies Commission, an outstanding committee of the National Education Association, has this to say of the bulletin; "It is probably the most influential educational document issued in this country." The commission, in its The Purposes of Education in American Democracy, then goes on to restate or reclassify the objectives of education.

This commission lists four major objectives: (1) The objective of self-realization, which covers in general the same area as covered by health, command of fundamental processes, worthy use of leisure, and ethical character of the seven cardinal principles group; (2) The objective of human relationship, which deals with members of the family and community group and is akin to worthy home membership, citizenship, and worthy use of leisure of the seven cardinal principles objectives; (3) The objective of economic efficiency, which covers in general the same area as vocational preparation and worthy home membership; and (4) The objective of civic responsibility, which is essentially the same as the objective of citizenship in the seven cardinal principles group. Since physical education is a part of education, it has the same general goals. The closeness of this relationship can be shown by pointing out the numerous ways in which physical education contributes to these goals.

Major Contributions to Health

These contributions can be made to both physical and mental health. The proper functioning of the social life of the individual is considered under ethical character and citizenship. Health is considered as that condition, mental and physical, in which the individual is functional, well adjusted internally as concerns all body parts and externally as concerns his environment.

Physical exercise and development of the muscular system have furnished an incentive to develop the other body systems in the advance from the lower to the higher forms of life.

In the amoeba, the simplest form of animal life, the one cell carries on all of the functions of the organism. Living in water, it gets nourishment by absorption from particles around which it wraps itself; in this process there is a secretion which helps digestion. Excretion is simply unfolding and moving away from the waste products remaining. As a means of locomotion it throws out a pseudopodium and rolls and drags itself over toward it; one piece is extended and the remainder of the cell then works over to it. Respiration is performed by absorbing oxygen from the water through the surface of the cell. There is no true circulation-the process is about like the diffusion of bluing in water.

There is no known nervous system, but if the amoeba is properly stimulated it responds. Reproduction takes place by division of the cell into two; these two in turn divide to produce others.

The sponge, a slightly higher from of life, has specialized reproduction cells and a skeleton, but otherwise shows no great functional advance over the one-celled amoeba except in the combination of cells.

The hydra, a coelenterate, shows functional advancement in that it has crude muscles and nerves and gets nourishment from "outer surface" cells.

In the earthworm we note a marked advancement over the hydrainage regard to functional systems. It has a co-ordinated muscular system which provides for locomotion. The energy necessary for even the relatively slow movement of the worm is immense as compared to the amount required in the life process of the practically immobile hydra. The extra muscle needed to move the worm about must be maintained during periods of inactivity as well as during times of action.

The hydra not only does not need to provide the energy for appreciable motion but is entirely free from the task of supporting a muscle mass of any consequence. With this gradually increasing muscle mass, requiring proportionately more nourishment, the developing worm is faced by a great problem; some better method of securing food than taking it through the outer skin must be provided. The answer to this problem is the development of a digestive tract or long hollow tube with some secretory tubes along the sides of it—a marked advance toward a digestive system. The worm is divided into numerous small segments, united end to end. Each segment has two primitive kidneys for excretion, and the whole organism has an outlet for waste other than the body surface.

A circulatory system is developed to carry food to the cells and waste products away from them. By no means the least important addition is the directing or nervous system, which controls and regulates all other systems. In the worm there are separate nodes for each section and a larger or more important ganglion in the head section. These various centres exhibit a rough kind of teamwork in action. A special reproductive unit is in evidence here too. Of those body systems that are primarily concerned with the individual's own life, the muscular system is the oldest and furnishes the main reason for the others' existence. However, the muscles existing in the earthworm compare only to our trunk and neck muscles; our other muscle groups came later. This phylogenetic development might be traced on up the scale of life, showing how the various parts originated. The muscles comparable to our shoulder and hip muscles appeared at the time of the fish; those of the arms and legs at the amphibian stage; and so on until the development of the hand muscles, which first appeared in the primates.

It must be remembered that although it came into being in a rudimentary form in the reptile, one of the very last regions to develop in its great complexity was the cerebral cortex, which develop in its great complexity was the cerebral cortex, which developed almost concurrently with the nerves and centres controlling the limbs and the delicate hand co-ordinations. The muscles and nerves that are phylogenetically old are larger, stronger, and less complex than those that are not so old.

These large-muscle groups with their controlling nerves are called the fundamental groups in that they came first or are phylogenetically older and are basic units. Those structures and functions which developed later—the cortex, the smaller muscles of the arms and legs, and vocalization—are called the accessory groups, because they are developed later as structural and functional additions to the earlier fundamental units. It seems to be a rule in nature that an adequate functioning of the fundamental groups is essential to a proper functioning of the more recently added accessory structures. That is, long continued proper functioning of the cortex depends upon exercise of the large muscles, particularly during the growing period. Before birth, ontogeny roughly repeats phylogeny as far as the physical organism is concerned. There is some small evidence of this trend after birth. The nervous system and the brain, however, develop relatively early, and growth of the various body parts is anything but uniform in progress; but when a system is started, it follows crudely the life history of the race. There is far less evidence of recapitulation after birth than before, for it is in attitudes, urges, and mental condition that the implied recapitulation takes place, and accurate evidence concerning attitude and urges is difficult to obtain.

The hypothesis advanced here is not that the specific physical changes are marked or noticeable, but that the general plan is followed; that, since big muscle action has ushered in progress of the various organic systems in the racial past, the plan is still used for proper development of those systems during the individual's growth. Nature discards very slowly the principles, constructions and devices that have, at some time, proven useful. Physical exercise and a great deal of it, is advocated as one of the necessary means of attaining a healthy development.

The child who exercises plentifully becomes tired and will rest better; gets hungry and will eat more; has more need of oxygen, and breathes more deeply and more rapidly; has more waste content to be carried from the cells and needs more nourishment for the cells, causing increased circulation; all of these contribute their bit toward better elimination of waste. This concentration on the other functions of the body strengthens the higher and lower directing centres, which are responsible for all action, but it does not require great action of the cortex. This is as it should be, for in youth the cortex is not ready to respond to extreme demands.

There are three fairly well differentiated stages of growth gradually leading from the first to the last; pure growth, developmental growth, and approaching maturity. During the period of pure growth, which is almost entirely an increase in mass, practically no exercise is needed. About all of the body parts except the cortex and some of the accessory muscles have passed through that stage at birth, and are ready for developmental growth, which should include increase in both mass and function but should not undergo intense exercise. The cortex is still so close to the pure growth stage for some time that only a small amount of exercise is needed. Any effort to improve upon the original plan an rush the developmental process is apt to produce harmful results, in terms of chorea, nervousness, and similar disturbances. Experimenters have used tadpoles in testing out the proposal that nature can be hurried along. Since the tail is absorbed to be replaced by hind legs, anyway, the tails of some were cut off in an effort to hurry the appearance of the hind legs. The hind legs did develop sooner than in the non-mutilated tadpoles, but they were deformed.

The penalty for violation of the general developmental principle was deformity. This experiment offers guiding advice to those who would neglect the physical and rush mental development. The third stage of growth is that of approaching maturity when marked activity is necessary to finish off properly the functional growth of the various parts. In general, the large-muscle groups are one stage ahead of the cortex and of the accessory groups in terms of development. In case of any doubt, it is safe to allow and advise additional physical, and less cortical, activity during childhood. Our present generation is nervous and unsettled. What can be expected of the next if concentration on cortical activity crowds out still more of the physical? This line of reasoning can be advanced one step further.

The other body systems still depend upon the action of those same muscle groups for stimulation to proper functioning during adult life. However, the amount of exercise required is much less than was needed in the first few years of life. This reduction in amount of required exercise has been taking place gradually. As the cortex reaches the more advanced stages of growth, it can stand more exercise and consequently should have more. In adult life, or even earlier, it has completed the period of developmental growth and more of the time of education can be devoted to "mental pursuits." This does not mean that physical activity is no longer necessary but, rather, that the body needs proportionately less exercise as age advances. Those who have neglected the physical and concentrated on the mental have suffered. It is the office workers and other men who use their cortex and inner hand muscles to the neglect of the large-muscle groups who have nervous breakdowns, rather than the day labourer, who exercises chiefly his large-muscle groups. These phylogenetically young members of the total body equipment, the interpretative and emotional controls of the cortex, and the fine hand co-ordinations, are the weaker ones in terms of stability and endurance.

They are the ones that give way first in the presence of sudden, immediate strain and also under long continued strain. Exercise of the older groups seems to build up strength in the new or to recharge them. The human system may be likened to a motor vehicle in regard to certain functional purposes, provided the analogy is not pressed too far: let the engine, or motive power, represent the large-muscle groups, and the battery, with its control over the lights and starter, represent the cortex. Assuming normal functioning conditions, then long driving or use of the engine charges the battery, strengthens the starter, and furnishes plenty of electricity of the lights. Suppose, however, that the lights are left on and the engine is started often but very little driving is done. After a time the battery will not be strong enough to start the engine and the lights will be dim. It is much the same with college students who neglect the physical in an effort to concentrate upon the mental. The average undergraduate does not suffer much, but the graduate student who is convinced that since he is a man in the realm of academic advancement he must put away may of the childish things of the undergraduate, including exercise, is very apt to suffer., Hence we conclude that physical education contributes to physical and mental health through the use of the fundamental muscles, which stimulate action of the other body systems and tend to "charge the cortical battery." Physical education contributes in other ways also. School children need some joyous excitement and will have it. Activity can substitute for dissipation, delinquency, and carousing by giving youngsters something interesting to do. Free time, once spent on playgrounds, on hikes, in gymnasiums, or in other areas of physical activity, is used up and hence cannot be spent in some unfavourable environment.

The evidence indicates that juvenile delinquency decreases as supervised play areas increase in number. Team games provide an excellent means of keeping certain youngsters' mind off sex matters. Especially at the adolescent age there is much dreaming and planning about things that appeal. In many unfortunate cases this centres around sex. With adequate direction, the team and its success can become the centre of plans, dreams, and activity; and, thanks to the much maligned coach, they often do! Then, too, vigorous play tires the growing boy, and his bed becomes a place for sleep rather than one for sleep and day dreaming. Students acquire sound habits only by practice, not by reading or hearing about them. Athletics, a large part of physical education, contributes well to health in this respect.

In order that the individual may be a better player

now, or at some time in the future, he will gladly practice health habits. He will avoid some stimulants and poisons, establish regular and sufficient hours of sleep and rest, select more carefully the foods he eats, and, in general, practice better habits of living. We must never forget the value of play as mental relaxation.

It takes the youngster's mind off his worries and troubles; it provides a change in the emphasis of his concentration. Something new and vital to think about provides mental rest just as change of occupation provides physical rest. When we realize that one half of the hospital beds in the United States are occupied by mental cases, the importance of the mental aspect of health becomes readily apparent. During adolescence especially, but during young generally, there are emotional stresses and strains brought on by the conflicts between one's own plans and actions and the plans and actions of others. This emotional tension, flavoured with anger, fear, and the other strong emotions, provides increased internal secretions of adrenaline and the like.

It is better to work off the products normally through vigorous activity than it is to force the vital organs to make the adjustment of returning to the normal condition without the aid of such big-muscle activity. There is relatively clear evidence to the effect that exercise carried to the extent of marked fatigue leaves an individual more susceptible to certain diseases than he would have been without the exercise. However, competent physical educators discourage the practice of exercising to the point of extreme fatigue just as they do other excesses. The loss of resistance to infection is partially compensated for by the fact that regular, adequate exercise builds one up to the place where he is less readily fatigued. Then, when emergencies arise which demand an extra output of physical activity, he will be less fatigued than he would have been had he not build up his endurance. By practice the threshold of fatigue can be raised through developing greater endurance.

Contribution to the Attainment of Fundamental Processes.

The point here is to support the contention that there are "fundamental processes" in physical education; once this is established it is readily apparent that physical education contributes to their attainment. Those fundamental processes are the physical skills common to America in general and to one's own locality in particular.

They are fundamental chiefly because the child needs them now for happy living, but also because future physical education endeavours and many life occupations are based upon them. As was pointed out before, children live on a different level from that of adults. In play situations the good performer is the hero and the poor performer is pushed into the background. Much of child life is play life, and a large share of it deals with physical sills; whereas only a small part of adult life is play, and good performance is not stressed so much. If an adult loses at golf or does poorly in a ball game at a picnic, it matters little, for success in those areas is not particularly vital; there are many other things that influence happiness so much more.

The child does not have those numerous other phases of endeavour to which he can turn for success if he fails miserably in his physical skills. He must master the fundamental processes or suffer the consequences of loss of standing and recognition among his fellows in one of the major fields of youthful endeavour. That is one of life's most severe punishments, and it can be avoided by improving physical abilities. Many unhappy, insignificant boys have become leaders in their school because of improvement in their fundamental skills. Whether boys and girls go on to college or into other walks of life, training in the fundamental skills is necessary.

It is unpleasant and unprofitable to remain below the elementary school athletics and leisure-time sports activities demand a thorough grounding in the fundamental physical activities and skills. Certainly physical education contributes largely to the attainment of an adequate command of may of the important fundamental educational processes.

Contribution to Ethical Character, Worthy Home Membership, and Good Citizenship.

Since many of the qualities that make for achievement in any one of the above provide for achievement in the other two, the three are grouped together. Health, which helps to a larger degree in attaining worthy home membership and citizenship and less in attaining ethical character, is any exception worth noting. Physical education is one phase of school work that lends itself particularly to the development of character. Student interest prevails, activity is predominant, and relatively great authority and respect are accorded those in charge.

The physical education class provides more than

just a place to discuss character education theory; it furnishes a laboratory for actual practice. We develop character much more surely by living it out than we do by hearing about what should be done or should not be done. It is one matter to decide upon the correct response to a tense situation when merely looking on, and an entirely different proposition to decide and act correctly when in the midst of heated combat. One contestant may foul another, unnoticed by the official, near the end of a close game and thous prevent an opportunity to score. The player fouled cannot take his ensuing action under advisement and decide some time later what to do about it. He must decide at once and give his answer immediately by what he does.

This splendid educational laboratory demands actual responses to tense situations just as much as life in general does. The whole setup provides real rewards and punishments which with proper guidance will serve to encourage sportsmanship, co-operation, sociability, self--control, leadership, and those other qualities of character and citizenship which we stress. The competitor is an active citizen, not a passive one. It is the acting citizen who receives training. There are lows or rules that must be obeyed as he drives on toward his major ambition of winning the contest or performing well. There are penalties imposed immediately upon any infraction of the law. Opportunities to give, to take, to obey, and to co-operate are numerous. Here is the ideal setting for developing the good citizen, the worthy home member and the individual of ethical character, provided, of course, that the situation is well handled and well regulated. In no school situation are the goals adequately attained if those in charge are incapable or indifferent. As in the case of health, the dominant drive for a winning team or good performance leads to the development of good habits. Sane character habits, such as controlled sex life and abstinence from the use of alcohol, are steps in the direction of good citizenship that can be prompted by athletic competition. In order that he may be a better player, the youngster will practice these and other habits of good citizenship. In the long run as well as in the immediate situation, clean living builds for success. Habits of clean living and good citizenship tend to carry on just the same as do undesirable habits. Enough good ones crowd out some bad ones. Out personality with its basis of character is, after all, the sum total of our responses to the social situations in which we find ourselves. We establish characteristic reactions to familiar situations. Pursuit of interesting, desirable goals during the period of habit formation will help to develop desirable reaction patterns.

It may be unreasonable to contend that the boy who displays co-operation and consideration in game situations will ask a tired mother to permit him to do the dishes in the evening: it is probable that he sees no common elements in these situations. All good traits certainly will not carry over completely from one situation to another; but, if there are many, at least a few may be expected to carry over to similar situations. When all other phases of school life contribute their bit toward good citizenship, worthy home membership, and ethical character, generalizations of fairness, sportsmanship and the like can be build up that will have some carry-over value. The identical elements involved should also carry over to similar home and community situations. Some of the skills learned contribute to worthy home membership and citizenship as well as they do to command of the fundamental processes. Other things being equal, the more skilful home member is more worthy than the less skilful one.

Contribution to the Worthy Use of Leisure.

Within the last 30 years, the hours of labour for children and adults have been drastically reduced. Many informed people predict further reduction. Whether or not this anticipated reduction comes to pass, there is a vast amount or leisure time to be spent now; much more than ever before in the history of this country. It is not during the hours of labour that unsocial conduct develops but in the hours of relaxation and freedom. Since it is during free or play time that those who enter crime prepare for that regrettable adventure, steps must be taken to employ that time more profitably. It is to this phase of guidance and development that physical education is eminently qualified to contribute. It is provides a means of interesting, active, and constructive adventure instead of an approach to unsocial conduct. Inherently youth desires physical activity, competition, co-operation, fellowship, and many of the other elements in our program. It is well to note that adequate provision for the leisure time of adolescents is more important than is the preparation for their leisure time when they will be adults.

If the problem is adequately administered in youth, there will be little cause for anxiety about it during the time of adult life. It is a mistake, then, to criticize many of our more vigorous team games on the count that they do not provide carry-over activities for later life; they do not need to do that in order to justify themselves for they serve the cause of leisure time right now. In meeting the leisure needs of youth, they may render a greater service than those less vigorous games which carry over into adult life. One reason for this lies in the fact that children have much more free time than adults: the greater need offers the greater opportunity for service. Another reason which has been touched upon above, is that proper training and correct habit formation in youth may carry over into adult life. Adult habits cannot revert to a youth that is past.

It is most valuable to occupy the leisure hours and days of youth harmlessly and constructively. Since team games attract strongly, they have the power to pull youngsters to them who might not be attracted otherwise. To be sure, our games that have carry-over value as entire games into adult life need to be included among the physical activities of adolescents, but they must not be used to the exclusion of the more vigorous team games. It may even be possible that one will grow tired of a game that is made to serve regularly for both young and adulthood. Since we have so generally accepted tennis, golf, skating, swimming, handball, and other sports of the nature as valuable units in a program that purports both to provide and to prepare for leisure time, they need not be defended here.

Physical education is not presented as the only unit in the school system that contributes to the worthy use of leisure but as one of the important units that has a significant contribution to mark, both during the school age and later in life.

Contribution to Vocational Preparation.

Better physical and mental health, character, and

citizenship will aid one in securing and maintaining employment. The endurance, strength, and skills developed in physical activities increase one's efficiency in many types of work. Certain types of physical activity, notably athletic games, develop leadership and poise. These are always vocationally valuable. Studies spaced over the past 25 years tend to show that those who won letters on varsity athletic teams in colleges and universities have had greater success in life, measured in terms of financial and social achievements, than did their classmates who were not letter winners in sports.

This is to be expected, since the letter winners had more directed or guided opportunities through which to pursue the total objectives of education than did the remainder of the student bodies from their respective institutions.

4

Administrative Policies & Activities

Any department that is to function adequately must have sound, well-established administrative policies, or guiding rules, as a basis on which to operate. Policies, unlike objectives, usually indicate the method of approach or means or procedure rather than the point to be gained. It is not enough to struggle along solving problems as they arise. Conditions may make it possible to go through the motions of conducting a department by this resort to lame expedients, but sound administration demands a positive, planned procedure rather than a floundering makeshift.

It is essential that all staff members, as well as the director, know the policies which are to serve as guides. Staff friction often arises because there is a difference of opinion regarding authority and responsibility or accepted procedure. When all persons concerned know that one way rather than another is the accepted method of procedure, conflicts between two reasonably sound courses of action will be reduced to a minimum. It should be evident to any student of administration that local conditions will influence policies, and that under certain circumstances administrative policies will be called for which differ materially from equally sound policies found applicable under other conditions. The policies presented below and discussed at length later in this chapter purport to cover the field adequately but not to condemn similar fundamental ideas stated in a different manner. Although presented from the viewpoint of a larger departmental organization, the following policies can be modified without much difficulty to apply to smaller school.

It is readily apparent that a number of the policies do not apply in situations where one member constitutes the entire department. Generally, administrative problems increase as the size of the department increases, or, starting with a large department, decrease as the department decreases in size. This means fewer policies for smaller departments. Policies are developed through experience of both the policy maker and others. In any case, trial application in the local situation may eliminate, modify, or establish prospective policies.

Guiding Policies

There are six major policies under which are grouped the more specific explanatory policies. The director should:

1. Be just to his students.

(a) Give grades for work in physical education.

(b) Provide for an extensive rather than an intensive

program.

(c) Provide for student leadership and responsibility.

(d) Keep the gymnasium, service units, and play areas clean and sanitary.

(e) Provide the most adequate and workable scheme of classification of students possible.

(f) Take care of injuries suffered in athletic competition.

(g) Provide towels and adequate protective equipment for ragged activities.

(h) Teach skills and games useful in school and in later life to non-athletes as well as athletes.

(i) Require a medical examination of all participants in physical activities.

2. Insofar as possible operate on the basis of facts.

(a) When he performs an executive act, take steps immediately to collect facts which will enable him to appraise the effect of the act.

(b) Before setting up a policy, secure the facts which will provide a defensible basis.

(c) Ask for support of policy only if facts point toward the desirability of the procedure; one should not ask for support on a personal basis.

3. Be just to his staff..

(a) Delegate authority and responsibility clearly.

(b) Inform staff members concerning openings in other institutions.

(c) Reward and encourage the contribution of ideas and service by the staff.

(d) Provide a reasonable teaching load.

(e) Require all members to be qualified for their positions.

(f) Stress staff selection rather than dismissal as a way out of staff troubles.

(g) Meet with the staff to discuss policies and procedures, especially any tentative plans affecting them.

4. Be just to the educational system.

(a) Co-operate rather than contend with other departments.

(b) See to it that pursued aims and objectives are in accord with those of education.

(c) Refrain from embarrassing faculty members by asking special favours for athletes.

5. Be just to the public.

(a) Keep the department well represented in all worthwhile civic organizations.

(b) Keep the public continually informed about the educational work that is being done.

(c) Operate on a sound financial basis; have a budget and follow it.

6. Be just to his opponents and competitors.

(a) Seek the advice of opponents.

(b) Regulate the crowds at athletic contests so that both teams may compete under favourable conditions.

(c) Join an athletic conference.

In view of the fundamental importance of these major policies and sub-policies, they are discussed in greater detail in the following paragraphs:

1. Be just to his students.

(a) It the science instructors of any school blessed with a splendid laboratory for physics or chemistry were to make no provision for student use of it, they would be justly criticized. Because of the nature of its program and the instinctive urges of the pupils the physical education department has a splendid laboratory for developing social qualities, especially leadership Those in charge are under as much obligation to use it as are the instructors in charge of a science department to use their laboratory. Such use should provide opportunities for students to assume responsibility and to share leadership in number of the activities on the program under competent guidance. The incentives to achieve are fundamental and strong, the rewards are satisfying, and action predominates. The leader is the man of action who can command in critical situations. Physical education can easily provide many of these situations for developing leadership and responsibility. Any department that fails to do this is not fulfilling its obligations to its students.

(b) There are very definite limits established in most schools beyond which the classifying students on the basis of academic ability is the major factor that limits school-wide classification for physical education purposes, because groups cannot be broken down and reformed for each type of activity; the would involve insurmountable schedule making difficulties. A wide variety of abilities indifferent activities and relatively few easily applied good tests also limit the scope of classification. It is possible, however, to classify within the actual class in most schools, and within the same grade in some schools. This should be done where possible because in this way physical education can be made more truly educational.

(c) Physical education is one of the educational subjects, and its standing can be established and maintained more adequately by offering the same academic rewards as are offered in other departments for the same excellence of achievement. There will be more incentive to achieve if rewards are commensurate with achievement, than if the students who really work get the same meaningless "Cr." as other students who merely put in an appearance. Grading will make for a better teaching situation and provide a means of interesting a better qualified personnel. As the instructors and students improve, the program will appeal more to the taxpayers, and they will be more willing to support it. By giving grades, a department of physical education puts itself in a position to offer better service.

(d) The offering in physical education should include activities that are useful during the time that participants are in school as well as after their school days are over. It is entirely possible that a number of activities can serve both purposes well. There are some, however, that will serve better during school days, such as football and basketball, and others which customarily, although not of necessity, serve more generally at a later time. Handball and volley ball are games of this type. Some departments overemphasize the games most interesting and useful during school days, others "go to seed" by sponsoring predominantly those activities which will serve better later in life. Both must be included in a balanced program.

(e) Every normal student in school has the right to expect that interesting physical activities and facilities for enjoying them will be provided for him or her. It is a mistake to expect all students to fit into the mould formed by a few popular physical activities. It is also impossible to provide facilities for every type of activity that any student might desire; but it is entirely possible and reasonable to provide a variety of activities, rather than to concentrate on a few. Inclusion of as large a sampling as the institution can afford and direct should be a goal for every department. By means of this comparatively extensive offering each student has the opportunity of selecting the activities which he enjoys. This policy is in direct opposition to the regulation, not uncommon in colleges and universities, that all students must learn to swim. This old fallacy seems to be built on the supposition that those who can swim will be able to save themselves from drowning when the emergency arises. The facts, often overlooked, are that many good swimmers drown, that a goodly number of people are never put in the position where they need to swim, that swimming may increase sinus and ear infection in certain cases, and that it is often decidedly unpleasant for those who have difficulties in learning. This unpleasantness amy create a dislike for physical education. This is not a condemnation of swimming, which is splendid activity, but a condemnation of the policy of requiring it of all students. There is no one sport or other activity in which proficiency should be required of all; choice rather than specific requirement marks the progressive activity program. It should be pointed out here that the instructor should give the best he has to every student, whether or not he is a varsity athlete or ever has a chance to be come one.

(f) There are many youngsters as well as adults who are not aware of their own serious ailments. There are still others who will try to keep any information about such a weakness a secret if they have reason to believe that its discovery will deprive them of participation in some favoured activity. There is still a third group that will feign illness or an abnormality in an attempt to avoid physical exercise which they probably need very badly. In order that a department may operate with accurate knowledge of the condition of the pupils and thus reduce permanent injuries or even fatalities, a medical examination is necessary. This examination should be given before activity classes or groups meet. Only the careless or inefficient instructor will be satisfied with the examination given at just any time during the semester. The preliminary inspection may be made by the school nurse or some instructor, but the examination proper should be made by a doctor of medicine. It is unwise and may even be dangerous for the coach or physical education instructor to assume a doctor's duties unless he is a physician.

(g) Certain types of athletic competition are apt to result in injuries, such as breaks, bruises, abrasions, sprains, and dislocations. Since some of the participants will not receive treatment unless the school provides it, it is the responsibility of each educational institution to furnish this service. Lack of funds, carelessness, a false belief in the virtue of being able to endure injuries, or fear of parental disapproval of the activity through which this injury was sustained may lead to non-treatment of the injury if the matter is left to the student's initiative. Since the school sponsors interesting, although rigorous, activities, it must take care of the accidents that happen as a result of participation if it is to be just to those who engage in them.

(h) No school has a right to expect or require students to engage in activities or to dress for and bathe after the activities, under dirty and unsanitary conditions. If physical education is to maintain and promote health, the least that can be expected of the department is cleanliness and sanitation sufficient to prevent the spread of disease and infection. That meagre minimum is not really adequate, for education at its best is conducted in pleasant surroundings; it even gains in effectiveness because of an excellent environment. Respect and appreciation are instilled most thoroughly through example. When those in charge show by the condition in which they keep the plan that they respect and appreciate it, then those who come to learn will have similar feelings for the physical equipment and the program that is offered there.

(i) In some situations it is not possible to provide adequate equipment for certain rugged activities. When that condition exists, those activities should not be sponsored by the institution, for sever injuries often result because of inadequate protective equipment. There will be pressure at times from some community groups for certain activities. If the activities are acceptable, those in charge should work toward providing the necessary equipment and even let the community sponsors help secure the equipment, but should refrain from engaging in the activities until it is provided. It is often difficult to keep individually furnished towels clean or even available when they are needed; for that reason it is advisable for the school to furnish towels whenever possible. In many situations it is easier to renounce any responsibility in this matter than it is to plan and carry through a campaign to secure towels, a place to keep them, and an individual to care for them. However, the entire program will function more satisfactorily as a general rule if this service is provided.

2. Insofar as possible operate on the basis of facts.

(a) It may be necessary from time to time to modify or even replace established policies, but there will be little need of this if the supporting facts for each policy are at hand before it is adopted. If policies are formed predominantly on the basis of trial and error, more modifications and replacements will be found necessary. This limitation need not eliminate the use of hunches or inspirations; it merely insists upon a thorough checkup on the idea before trying to put it into practice. Time and effort spent in collecting information on a procedure, apparently sound upon preliminary consideration, will prove to be undesirable after a more thorough investigation of its implication. For example, a sub-policy concerning insurance of football players might be proposed, but before the wisdom of such a procedure can be determined many facts must be collected. The cost of insurance, the size of the squad, the cost of caring for injuries without insurance, and the amount paid through insurance in event of injury will all help provide the answer. Until those facts are known, the administrator cannot justifiably accept or reject the proposal. At times, temporary policies need to be established before the facts concerning them are available; however, such cases are infrequent. Except in those rare cases the facts should be collected first and the policies should be based on them.

(b) Every administrator make some decisions on the spur of the moment and others after but cursory consideration. After the decision has been made or the executive act has been performed, steps should be taken immediately to collect the facts which will enable one to appraise the consequences of the act. At times it is necessary to go beneath the surface to the act. At times it is necessary to go beneath the surface to find the real facts, for things may be apparently satisfactory but actually undesirable. The sublime confidence that all is well may be rudely shaken by the jarring of harsh facts. Since it is better to find out for one's self before too much damage has been done than to wait for complaints or friction to call mistakes to one's notice, it is necessary to get the evidence concerning the results of significant executive acts.

(c) It is difficult, but necessary, because of the unreliability of judgment when strongly favoured with emotional content, to eliminate or reduce to the minimum the personal prejudices or desires that influence policy formation. Cursory observation of the display of parental fondness, bordering on ecstasy, at the normal actions of an average, first-born baby offers evidence of the power of emotions over calm judgement. To illustrate further, the old home place is often beautiful to those who have many pleasant memories built around that cherished spot, but only ordinary to the stranger. It is fortunate indeed that feelings of appreciation can make the commonplace beautiful and extremely worthwhile. However, those unacquainted with the personal feelings which have influenced policy formation will note only the mediocrity that results and will judge accordingly. At best, a weak policy is still weak in spite of personal preference for it, and it is generally recognized that a policy can serve only according to its strength.

3. Be just to his staff.

(a) One of the well-established principles of applied psychology is succinctly stated in the law of effect. This law declares that other things being equal, the individual tends to repeat those responses which are satisfying and to avoid those which produce annoyance. Every member of a staff has many possibilities for service to the department that can be stimulated into usefulness if he is given sufficient incentive to exert himself. The law of effect applies in this situation as in ordinary learning situations; stimulation and encouragement will bring about valuable suggestions and outstanding services. By the same token, indifference and destructive criticism will as certainly limit or eliminate valuable suggestions and additional services. No outstanding department can be maintained without the helpful suggestions and volunteer services of most of its members. The enthusiasm which comes when one feels one's self a significant part of the organization often prompts heretofore neglected members to rise from mediocrity to excellence. Appreciation of suggestions and efforts made by members helps to create the feeling of "really belonging."

(b) One of the most severe, yet justifiable, condemnations of physical education today is the contention that those who teach it are not adequately prepared. Several states have special physical education certification requirements and more are adopting them. This fact will help decidedly in putting the physical education program into the hands of a prepared personnel. In the absence of specific certification requirements each school system should require ample preparation of prospective candidates for the positions to be filled. For instance, if there is an imperative need for a coach who can win games, an well prepared prospect should be selected, for there are men of that type available. In many, although not all, smaller communities, teachers are selected because of their ability to teach academic subjects or to coach some sport, and then the most likely person is assigned to teach the remainder of the physical education program. Poorly taught physical education classes are almost certain to result, since the one selected may have little or no training for this additional work. As the community becomes aware of this inefficiency there is a loss of faith in physical education class work and, consequently, an unwillingness to support it. In this way physical education maintains a position of insignificance in many communities because of any untrained personnel. Even in larger communities no staff member should be hired just for the sake of friendship, for that is unfair to the department and to the trained members of staff. If physical education is to progress, it must do so under the guidance of a well trained personnel.

(c) There is not more important phase of administration than that of selecting a staff, for it is the staff that puts the program into operation and maintains its proper functioning. That portion of a director's budgeted time and effort which is to be devoted to personnel replacements should be expended very largely before actual hiring takes place. Ultimately, this procedure requires less time and is decidedly more pleasant, because it reduces the number of replacements by decreasing dismissals, with their accompanying unpleasantness and implied condemnations. Wise selection requires a thorough understanding of the general and specific qualifications for each staff position, plus the ability to detect those qualifications, or their absence, in prospective members. This presupposes a competent department head who has thought through the entire program. It is hardly possible for a director who does not know just what he seeks to accomplish to select the proper staff to carry out efficiently a program to be determined at some later time. Each staff members employed and later dismissed by the same superior officer is to a certain extent a condemnation of the person who discharges him. He is also apt to be an enemy of the official who must make the decision which deprives him of his position, even though an honest effort is made to place him in a new position, even though an honest effort is made to place him in a new position. The emphasis should be decidedly upon selection rather than dismissal.

(d) The director should delegate authority and responsibility clearly. In order that misunderstandings may be reduced to the minimum, it is absolutely necessary to delegate clearly. The administrator who permits or encourages two different staff members to believe that they each have complete authority over one phase of the work, in order to avoid the unpleasantness that may result from telling one that he is subordinate to the other, is building toward discord and future trouble. The evil day may be postponed temporarily by this expedient, but it will be all the more violent when it does arrive. Lack of clear delegation of responsibility will provide an excuse for someone to avoid a portion of the unpleasant or arduous tasks, while other conscientious members will do more than their share. It should be pointed out particularly that delegation of responsibility should always carry with it delegation of authority. Anyone who is to be held accountable for a phase of the program must in all fairness have authority to act on matters concerning that unit. It would be no more unfair to hold a coach responsible for a team without granting him authority to conduct practice than it would be to expect any other staff member to produce result with out authority to proceed adequately in his area of operation.

(e) It is important to meet with the staff to discuss policies and procedures; to meet each member in private conference from time to time and to meet all as a group at regular intervals. Morale is developed, in part at least, by getting together and developing a unity of purpose. Many possible minor difficulties can be forestalled by working out different angels of problems together. Builders of enthusiasm know the value of group meeting. Several thousand supporters of a team while in their respective home could not develop the enthusiasm or unity of purpose that come from getting together in a pep-meeting. A truly great staff must have enthusiasm and unity of purpose, although of a somewhat different type from that of a football crowd. The director who becomes one of the staff, rather than someone apart from it, during the group meeting is building general staff support for the time when he may need it.

(f) Although but a small percentage of physical education staff members are teaching merely for the financial rewards connected with it, practically all of them need money in order to live in a society such as ours, and for that reason they are looking for positions that pay better salaries. Many are also looking for opportunities to rise in the profession even though the salary may not be increases. In order to be just to the staff members, the director should pass on to those who might be interested beneficial information concerning openings in other schools. This may at times deprive his staff of the services of a good instructor, but there are plenty of others who would be glad to work for that type of director. At any rate, staff members should be held through payment of adequate salaries and through their enthusiasm for the department which employs them, rather than by attempts to keep them in the dark concerning possible opportunities for advancement elsewhere. The practice of increasing wages only because some other institution will take an employee away unless it is done is a political procedure and is hardly worthy of an educational institution.

(g) Policies concerning teaching load are discussed.

4. Be just to the educational system.

(a) There are few civic organizations, institutions, or departments within institutions in the United States that do not have reasonably sound, forward-looking objectives. However, there are many that have such objectives but fail to attain them with any marked degree of success. Physical education departments are sometimes listed among this group; in fact, physical educators have been accused of having one set of objectives for theory purposes and another for practice. This charge is due in part to the fact that the most interesting and exciting phases of the program are displayed "in the front window," where all may see. The activities of other more protected and secluded departments are thus apt to continue unnoticed while their more evident theories are compared with physical education practices. It is unfair to compare one group's theory with another group's practice. However, in order that the disparity between theory and practice, which does exist in many situations, may be reduced to a minimum, physical education must see to it that the pursued aims and objectives are identical with the stated aims and objectives.

(b) Physical education is not a weak and sickly child in the academic family that needs special care and protection. Instead, it is a healthy, well-nourished member and can better maintain that position by living on a regular diet than by being pampered with sweets and titbits, in the form of gift grades and special privileges to athletes. This does not mean that the athlete should not have the same opportunities as other students; he certainly should, but he is not entitled to more. Real men are developed by meeting the tests of school and life squarely rather than by depending on special privilege. In terms of a lifetime the student who is passed because he belongs to a certain group is handicapped rather than benefited. For that reason those in charge of an educational unit will not ask for favour but for equal treatment. This will substantiate the principle which a department should make clear to its students-that no academic immunities are in order since others have not received them. Although this may mean the lose of a few games now and the, it will mean a definite gain in the matter of developing men and women, which is the true justification for any unit of an educational system.

(c) It is important to be a good citizen in the school family; to give as well as take in the matter of sharing facilities. By sharing within reason, a director will build general faculty good will which will help, especially in times of stress, in keeping the department functioning. Other departments will have certain scheduled events that are significant to them, and the director should, insofar as possible, avoid conflicts with those events and their purpose. It is advisable to attend faculty meetings, even though they are not particularly thrilling. By demonstrating that "co-operation" rather than "contention" characterizes the physical education department, the other school departments will be led to respond more readily with the same attitude. The entire school can educate more thoroughly if harmony prevails.

5. Be just to the public.

(a) The director should keep the public continually informed concerning the educational work being done. By this means those in charge may be able to remain long enough in a situation to carry out an educational program that is planned and partially under way. The parents of a community will co-operate in promoting a worth while program for their children if they know about it. They cannot know as much as they should unless they are regularly informed concerning the program. Experience teaches us that the public will support a star about whom it is constantly informed; it will do the same for a good program about which it knows. Any parental or general community support for an educationally sound physical education program for its boys and girls is a step in the direction of justice for the community.

(b) The school is one of the significant units in the socioeconomic life of any community, and the physical education department is one of the school units that deals most largely with the public. It the school, through its physical education department, is to serve the public best, its members must be acquainted with the other individuals in the community and have some common interests with them. As the individuals who comprise a community learn to know those in charge of the physical education program better, they will be more sympathetic to it and thus provide an opportunity for physical education to it and thus provide an opportunity for physical education to serve the community as a whole. Friendship toward a useful institution or part of an institution enables that institution to render more clearly its optimum service. There will be times when worthy community projects need the assistance that the physical education department can provide, and connection with community organizations will provide a knowledge of the needs as they arise.

(c) Until quite recently it has been common practice for many departments of physical education to send money according to the day-by-day, or week-by-week demands and then to turn to the school board at eh end of the year to make up the not infrequent deficit. That method of handling funds is not only inadequate, because those in charge hardly know where they stand financially, but also unfair to the public. The community has a right to expect that money devoted to conducting the physical education program will be provided for any spent according to a well-worked-out plan. Justice to those who pay the bills demands that there be a budget and that it be closely followed. Planned spending is usually more careful and conservative spending.

6. Be just to his opponents and competitors.

(a) Since the public is more generally interested in the physical education program which includes athletics than in any other phase of school work, a greater number of individuals in the community will develop strong emotional attitudes toward parts of this program and toward those who conduct it. Some of these attitudes will be favourable and some will be unfavourable. Those who attack are the opponents of those who sponsor and direct the program. The wise director will ask the advice of his opponents so that he may know more clearly what his own weaknesses are and how he can correct them. Some of our greatest benefactors are our most severe critics, if we will but profit by their suggestions. Advice from critics is only advice, just as is advice from personal friends-it is to be followed or ignored according to the wishes of the one who receives it. The wise director will also ask the advice of his critics in order that he may discover their weaknesses. He will avoid arguing with them on their weak points because points of difference are seldom cleared up through arguments, but he may explain certain points upon which they are apparently misinformed. Finally, the wise director will ask the advice of his opponents \in order to give them an opportunity to explode their ammunition in a rather harmless way or to decide that they don't care to use it at all. It satisfies some persons simply to "get it off their chests" or at least to have an opportunity to do so.

(b) Each school that participates in interschool

contests should join an athletic conference. Conference membership promotes understanding through developing acquaintance and establishing rules and regulations. Much of the petty quarrelling concerning some phases of Olympic competition could be eliminated if all nations had the same rules and regulations concerning the disputed points. Conference membership improves officiating through common interpretation of rules and established policies concerning the selection of officials. It simplifies the matter of schedule making and helps maintain an interest in the contests. All in all, it makes membership convenient and serviceable to one's competitors and one's own school.

(c) As physical education becomes more educational, visiting teams will be accepted as guests and accorded the treatment due guests. This condition prevails quite generally now among the players themselves, but the spectators, who really have less at sake, are more inclined to exhibit antagonism toward visiting teams. This is due almost entirely to the lack of spectator education. It requires effort and persistence to control crowds, but they can usually be controlled, if those in charge want to control them and will put forth an honest effort to do it. Much improvement has been made in spectator control, but booing is still prevalent enough in many situations to decrease the educational value of the whole procedure. The first step toward general improvement is to put one's won house in order; then others may be influenced to correct their unsatisfactory practices. This reform is certain to come; it is out responsibility and privilege to hasten the approach of that day.

Setting up the Physical Education Unit

The administrator has two important groups of tasks to perform-he must organize or set up the department, and he must administer it or see that it functions properly. Let us consider, first, those acts which are predominantly matters of organization. Those dealing with the functioning of the unit are considered. Since a large number of the activities listed are discussed at length elsewhere in this text, they will be dealt with very briefly in this connection.

It must be understood that the activities of small and large departments differ in degree more than in kind. In the smaller department more duties will need to be performed by the director, whereas in the larger one more duties and authority will need to be delegated to others. In interpreting the material presented, then, allowance should be made for the delegation of many duties in large departments and performance of those duties in small one. In setting up the physical education unit, there are a number of problems that must be solved. Many of them can well be attacked concurrently, whereas some should be solved before others are attempted, and still others can be worked out best after the foundation is laid. The first essential task is that of determining aims and objectives.

This includes gaining perspective and establishing the relationship in one's thinking between physical education and general education. If the budget dictates the program, as is often the case, it should receive prior consideration. If, however, the situation is fortunate enough so that the program can dictate the budget, then the program should be set up first. After considering the above matters, additional facilities or alterations in facilities can well be considered. By this time it should be apparent that certain Positions on the staff are key positions and that others are less significant. The authority and responsibility connected with each position should by clearly established in order that they may be delegated later, when staff appointments are completed. It should be noted here that the staff is to be selected last, to fit the specific situations, after other matters of organization have been considered. Since the matter of administrative relationships is not considered in other chapters, as are the other major problems involved in setting up the physical education unit, it is presented here. There are many plans of departmental organization which will work well provided the following fundamental considerations are maintained: (1) authority and responsibility are clearly delegated; (2) each individual is adequately prepared for his position; (3) multiple responsibility to others, especially for a specific task is reduced to the very minimum; and (4) co-operation is stressed and encouraged.

The plans of departmental organization showing administrative relationships are presented for large systems in charts on the following pages, but the general plan is the same for smaller ones, except that in the latter case many positions are combined into a few because of marked staff reduction. There is no universal agreement concerning the proper relationship between the health program, the intercollegiate athletic program, and what is commonly called the "physical education program" in institutions of higher learning. Consequently, two reasonably sound types of organization showing administrative relationships based on two of the characteristic philosophies are presented. Various combinations of these two types can be developed from the setups presented.

Even though there is probably more agreement, although by no means universal accord, concerning the relationship of athletics and the rest of the physical education program in a good-sized city school system. An unbroken line indicates direct authority and responsibility, a broken line indicates partial authority and responsibility. Co-operative activity is not indicated, for all members are expected to co-operate.

Marking the Physical Education Unit Function

After the organization has been set up, it is the responsibility of the administrator to see that it functions. In order to accomplish this, he will need to attend to a number of administrative and nonadministrative duties.

Predominantly Administrative Duties—Duties of this nature make up the greatest proportion of the administrator's workload. They include:

1. Inspecting and observing the condition of facilities and the functioning of the various activity units. The director should by all means know what is happening and under what conditions it is happening.

2. Securing employment opportunities for athletes. Each school group should provide legitimate assistance for those who need it, and the director and some able assistant are often best prepared to do that for the athletes.

3. Directing the registration of students. Appoint staff members to handle the details, but take care of unusual cases, check petitions, and be available for

suggestions at registration time.

4. Providing for and maintaining in operation a system of student managers as a means of developing leadership.

5. Scheduling classes or delegating this responsibility to some staff member.

6. Ordering equipment or arranging to have the business manager do so in co-operation with the coach or teacher who is to use ut.

7. Making budgets. This will require the administrator's approval, although the necessary information upon which it is based will probably be gathered by other staff members and compiled by the secretary.

8. Training his secretary and acquainting her with the way he wants things done.

9. Handling correspondence with a great number of people including faculty, students, other friends of the institution, officials, representatives from other institutions, and representatives of supply and equipment companies. His secretary should read and answer many letters on minor points concerning which she has been trained.

10. Conducting add attending meetings of various groups, including staff, general faculty, committees, athletic council, alumni, clubs, and other community groups, and hold student conferences.

11. Informing the public directly or through some assistant concerning the educational activities of the department.

12. Checking reports from staff members, students, and others after they have been summarized and arranged by his secretary. He must then follow up or set in operation the machinery to care for the significant needs indicated in the reports.

13. Scheduling events of checking the tentative schedules of events that are presented by various staff members.

14. Checking and making necessary minor alteration in the items listed under organization of the department.

Additional duties. Besides the duties connected closely with the functioning of the system, there are many which are not predominantly administrative but may need to be performed by the administrator. They include such matters as coaching, teaching, supervising instruction, writing for publication, making speeches doing research, attending chapel, serving as patron at social affairs, entertaining guests, and conducting physical examinations.

5

The Importance of Efficient Financial Management

The financial management of his department is one of the most important duties of the physical education administrator. Although the financial aspects of the service and intramural programs are not particularly difficult or time consuming, those of the interscholastic and intercollegiate athletic programs do entail considerable responsibility. Most physical education directors administer the interschool athletic programs and are therefore concerned with handling money, making all types of financial transactions, bookkeeping, and preparing budgets.

In handling these financial matters, simple and effective procedures are available and should be used. Any school official who receives and expends funds is expected to employ sound business methods. For him to do otherwise reflects adversely upon him. This situation prevails, regardless of the size of the institution or the amount of money involved. No teacher or administrator can afford to be careless or ignorant in handling public funds. Another reason why efficient financial management is important is that maximum benefit must be secured from the revenue available.

Most departments never have sufficient funds to provide all the desired service to students. Consequently, available resources must be wisely employed. Almost invariably those departments with the most serious financial problems use the most unbusinesslike procedures. This is particularly true of small high schools and colleges. Despite the great importance of this phase of their duties, few directors are prepared for the efficient financial administration of the physical education department when they first undertake it. The great majority of administrators learn by the trial and error method. Experience may be the best teacher; but it is an expensive teacher, particularly where finance is concerned. Large universities and colleges emphasize the importance of special training when they employ an expert to handle the business affairs of the intercollegiate athletic program. The director is frequently selected for his business ability. The professional physical education programs should make some provision to prepare physical educators for the financial responsibilities which they will encounter in their positions.

THE PHYSICAL EDUCATION BUDGET

In the great majority of schools the budget for the service and intramural programs is prepared separately from the budget for interschool athletic. In an extensive study Adams discovered that approximately 80 percent of secondary schools followed the practice of having a separate budget for the athletic program. When the physical education budget is submitted separately from the budget for interschool athletics, it is much easier to prepare because it is not concerned with the estimation of income and it does not involve the amount or variety of expenditures. In such instances the physical education director's duties are not appreciably different from those of the head of the physics or chemistry department. The interschool athletic program is the factor which accentuates the financial responsibilities of physical education administrators.

Source of Financial Support. In most high schools and colleges and universities the usual practice is to finance the service and intramural programs from the institutional budget. The service program is considered a part of the curricular offerings and, as such, is almost invariably supported from the regular school funds. Similarly, the cost of facilities and personnel for intramural athletics is almost always carried in the institutional budget. Quite frequently, however, the equipment and operating expenses come from the interschool athletic funds. This situation should not prevail because intramural athletics are an integral part of the physical education program and should be provided for all students as a desirable educational experience.

Steps in Preparing the Physical Education Budget.

The major items involved in the separate physical education budget are capital outlay, expendable equipment, and maintenance and repairs. These items should be included under these separate headings in the budget. The cost of capital equipment and maintenance and repairs is comparatively easy to estimate. Capital equipment includes all expenditures which increase the value of the school plant, such as additions of any kind to the grounds, buildings, or fixed equipment. A new backstop, tennis court, or shower room are examples of capital outlay. Maintenance and repair items include painting, refinishing, and repair of equipment. The first step in determining the expendable equipment needed for the following year is to take an inventory of what is on hand. This should be done as late in the school year as possible because the equipment will continue in use until classes are terminated for the summer. Ordinarily, it will be necessary to take inventory three or four months before the end of the school year.

In this case an estimate must be made of the amount of wear and tear of the equipment during the remainder of the school year. With experience this can be done quite accurately. In making the inventory it is important to classify the condition of all items of equipment. Some equipment will be new of almost new; other equipment will be in moderate condition; some items will need repair; and others should be discarded.

A careful inventory is of vital importance, since the request for new equipment is based upon it. It is not a responsibility to turn over to students, although students may assist with it. The next step is to determine the total amount and type of equipment which will be needed during the next school year. Analysis of budgets for previous years will indicate the amount of equipment normally required. This amount can be used as the starting point for determining over-all requirements. Changes in the number of students, departmental policies, or the nature of the service and intramural programs will increase or decrease this amount.

When the estimate of total equipment needed has been obtained, the amount of new equipment to be ordered will be the difference between what is required and what is left over. In making the estimate of what is needed the administrator should be certain to order an adequate amount.

It is better to err on the side of too much rather than too little equipment. This does not suggest padding the budget. It does suggest liberal rather than ultraconservative estimates. It is preferable to have a small amount of equipment left over at eh end of the year rather than to run short. After the budget has received the necessary approvals the equipment should be ordered. Practices vary in this regard. In some schools the physical education administrator is free to order whatever equipment he prefers so long as his total spending does not exceed the money allocated.

In other schools bids from several merchandisers must be invited. In this case the administrator must prepare detailed specifications of what he wants. When equipment is purchased in this manner, frequently, the type of equipment received is not what was wanted. Generally, the responsibility is the administrator's because he did not prepare the specifications in sufficient detail. In a department with several staff members it is advisable to solicit their advice before ordering new equipment. The different staff members may have had more experience with certain items of equipment than the administrator, and their recommendations may be very helpful.

THE ATHLETIC BUDGET

Support of Interschool Athletics—Interscholastic and intercollegiate athletics are usually supported in part from the institutional budget and in part from gate receipts and other sources of income. Although most schools include the salaries of coaches from the regular institutional budget and provide for the maintenance and operation of the athletic facilities, few institutions go so far as to appropriate funds to meet the current expenses of the athletic program. Jenne, in a study of cities with population over 100,000, founds that 10 of 72 cities did this. In a study of 2,125 secondary schools, Hughes and Schooler discovered that only 15 percent of the school districts were moving toward complete financing of the athletic program from tax funds.

Ideally, interschool athletics should be financed in the same way as any other school subject. The only justification for interscholastic and intercollegiate athletics is the significant educational experiences they provide. These experiences are so vital and important that they merit financial support from institutional funds. These values of athletics cannot be obtained if the program must be supported by gate receipts. Gate receipts and educational outcomes are incompatible objectives of interschool athletics. Experience has repeatedly demonstrated that athletics are conducted on a much higher plane if they derive their support from regular school funds. The reason for the failure of many school to finance athletics properly stems from the philosophy that only curricular activities are deserving of such support.

Athletics originated as extracurricular activities and in many schools are still considered in that category.

However, there is an increasing trend to regard athletics as an integral part of the school curriculum. In New York State, athletics by Board of Regents' action are a definite part of the physical education program of the schools and boards of education are empowered to provide financial assistance from regular school funds. The practice of expecting interschool athletics to be largely self supporting has led to most of the problems which have developed.

The amount of gate receipts is largely dependent upon the success of the teams. The effort to produce winning teams often results in undesirable educational practices. Most of these are involved in getting superior athletes into school and in keeping them eligible to play. The athletic program can never be educational in a desirable sense so long as it remains commercial. The following statement by Hughes and French relates to this matter:

So long as the program of competitive sports must depend for its very existence upon the direct financial support of the public, it is not unreasonable to expect that varsity athletics in such schools and colleges will reflected the public rather than the educational point of view.

Where this is the case, it can scarcely by hoped that athletics will attain perfection in the imperfect society which so profoundly influences their policies. If interscholastic and intercollegiate athletics are ever to reflect the education rather than the public point of view, they must first achieve financial independence.

The Educational Policies Commission strongly recommends that the complete costs of the interscholastic athletic program be paid out of general school funds. In some states this cannot be done until permissive legislation is passed. Such legislation should be initiated in those states where it is needed.

The results of financing interscholastic athletics entirely out of tax funds in one city are reported as follows:

1. Most football games are now played on week-end afternoons, with resulting decrease in such problems as vandalism and rowdyism.

2. Some of the hidden costs of public high schools athletic fees, are reduced for the student.

3. The high school program has ceased to be a commercial enterprise, dependent on gate receipts. Outside pressure for postseason, charity, all star, and curtain raiser games have been eliminated.

4. More adequate health and safety protection is accomplished by having fewer games and contests, avoiding play during inclement weather, providing safe equipment and safe transportation, and valuing the health of the participant above the winning of the game.

5. All schools within a system are assured of equal quality of equipment and supplies. Through central purchasing savings can be had.

Sources of Athletic Income in High Schools

Brammell made a study of the sources of income of interscholastic athletics. In a recent study Adams found the five most frequent sources of income were: (1) gate receipts, (2) board of education, (3) student activity fees, (4) season tickets, and (5) athletic association membership fees. A comparison of Brammell's and Adams' data shows a close agreement regarding sources of income for interscholastic athletics, despite the considerable interval of time between the two studies.

Gate Receipts—These two studies reveal the importance of gate receipts as a source of income. Football and basketball are the chief income producing sports, although even these are not operated at a profit in many small schools. The other interscholastic sports rarely produce a profit. Gate receipts should come predominantly from the adult public.

This is an accepted policy to keep admission prices for students at a minimum. Athletics are organized for the benefit of students, who should not be deprived of the opportunity to attend because of high admission prices. A small number of high schools admit all students free. Students should also be given priority when it is necessary to limit attendance at indoor athletic contest because of inadequate seating accommodations.

The philosophy that the interschool athletic program should be subsidized by the institution does not infer that gate receipts should be abolished. Although this measure has considerable merit it is too revolutionary to be practical at the present time. Gate receipts are not objectionable so long as they are incidental. Sufficient funds should be appropriated to insure the adequate operation of the program.

The gate receipts would then revert to the institutional budget. The income from gate receipts is used to purchase equipment for athletic squads, to pay costs of team trips, medical care, scouting, advertising, towels, laundry, awards, films, officials, and other operational expenses. In many communities deficits will be paid by the school district or from the student body funds. It is exceptional to require that the deficit be liquidated during the ensuing year.

Some schools are fortunate enough to have surpluses at the end of the year. Such surpluses are either carried over to succeeding years, transferred to the student body budget, or turned over to the school district.

Student Activity Fees—Another important source of income is derived from the student activity fee. A substantial majority of high schools have adopted a student activity plan to provide support for all student activities. Under this plan each student pays a prescribed amount-usually from $5.00 to $8.00—which entitles him to admission to all home athletic contests and to all other school functions for which there is a charge, such as school plays, concerts, and operettas. In addition, the cost of the student newspaper and the school annual is defrayed in whole or in part. Most schools also admit students from out-of-town institutions to athletic contests at a reduced rate upon presentation of the student body card.

Students who do not belong to the student activity association are usually admitted to home contests at a reduced fee. The income from student body fees is usually apportioned over the various student activities. The allocation may be made by the student council, a student activity board, or a committee which consists of representatives of the various activities. Various arrangements are made to collect the student activity fee.

In some schools the entire fee is collected in a lump sum early in the fall. In other the fee is paid on the instalment basis, such as 15 cents per week for each week of the school year of 25 cents per week until the activity ticket is paid for. Experience has demonstrated that it is better practice to have the activity ticket completely paid for before the basketball schedule is completed.

In the majority of schools the student activity plan is not compulsory. This plan, however, interests a larger percentage of students in the various activities than any other.

Student Athletic Association—In some schools each student is assessed a certain amount which entitles him to membership in the student athletic association. The coast of membership in the athletic association varies from $2.00 to $5.00 per year and gives the student the privilege of attending all home games. Membership may be required or optional. This method was quite popular a number of years ago but has bee replaced in many schools by the student activity plan.

Miscellaneous Sources—Many high schools find it necessary to resort to additional methods of raising money. In the smaller institutions, the revenue from gate receipts, school board appropriations, and student fees is often insufficient to meet all of the expenditures. In addition to the miscellaneous of income cited above by Brammell, funds may be raised by dances, operettas, concerts, carnivals, pageants, mistrial shows, a school circus, class socials, plays, moving pictures, and picnics.

These methods of raising money frequently prevent athletic deficits. Some schools find it necessary to use one or more of such methods annually. The chief objection to raising money in this way is that students spend too much time and effort upon the way is that students spend too much time and effort upon the particular activity. At times, also, these activities take an undue amount of the teachers' time. If these money-raising ventures are overdone, the public becomes resentful.

Type of Student Tickets

Regardless of the manner in which students pay for their home athletic events, most schools provide some type of season ticket for them. In some institutions, a ticket is used which is punched in the appropriate space for each contest. Other institutions use a booklet made up of detachable slips which are consecutively numbered.

The student's signature is one the cover of the booklet, and a space is provided on each slip for his signature. For each contest, a designated slip is detached from the booklet. For identification purposes, students may be asked to sign the slip, and the signature may be compared with that on the cover. Some schools attach small photographs to the season ticket or booklet to eliminate their use by others than students. Student tickets should not be transferable.

Sources of Athletic Income in Colleges and Universities.

In the institutions of higher learning the chief sources of athletic income are gate receipts, student athletic fees, activity tickets, and institutional appropriations. Additional sources of revenue may be contributions, subscriptions, concessions, programs, parking fees, rental, and radio and television broadcasting fees. Contrary to the popular impression, intercollegiate athletics in the great majority of institutions are not self-supporting. Were it not for substantial support from institutional budgets, most intercollegiate athletic programs could not continue.

The salaries of coaches and other personnel connected with athletics, as well as the expense of maintaining and operating athletic facilities, come from this source. It is generally expected that athletic income will be sufficient to cover such operating expenses as equipment, travel, medical care, laundry, and officiating. It is only in a relatively small number of institutions that the income is sufficient to cover all expenses of intercollegiate athletics without assistance from the institutional budget.

Even in these institutions a portion of the salaries of athletic personnel may come from the physical education budget if these staff members perform some services in the physical education departments. In some of these schools the gate receipts are sufficient to purchase new buildings and facilities which are used for physical education and intramural as well as intercollegiate athletic activities.

A number of the wealthier private colleges provide for the complete support of intercollegiate athletics in the general budget. All expenses are covered by appropriations. The athletic income is purely incidental and reverts to the institutional budget. Heave reliance is placed upon gate receipts in colleges and universities.

The bulk of these come from football and basketball. When these two sports must support themselves as well as most of the other sports and pay salaries and provide college buildings and equipment, a situation is created which invites overemphasis by those concerned with its direction and management. Intramural athletics are financed from the athletic budget in many institutions. Educators have been very critical of various uneducational aspects of intercollegiate athletics; yet they themselves are partially responsible for their existence.

If the heavy burden on gate receipts could be lightened by adequate financial support, athletics would become more valuable as an educational agency. Student fees help substantially in supporting the intercollegiate athletic program. Most schools find it necessary to require the students to purchase a season ticket or coupon book. The price varies from $10.00 to $20.00 for the school year. This fee permits the student to attend all home athletic contests and to purchase tickets for contests away from home at a reduced cost.

Concessions—The income-producing possibilities of concessions have rarely been appreciated in small school and colleges. In these smaller institutions, where the financial need is the greatest, the concessions are frequently overlooked or, if they are used, they are inefficiently operated. Professional teams and large university athletic departments have discovered that there is substantial revenue in concessions if they are properly handled. Concessions may be handled by the school itself or by an outside concessionaries. Within the school it may be operated by the physical education or athletic department, the athletic association, or by some student organization. When concessions are handled outside the school, the commissionaire should be selected after competitive bids have been received. In advertising bids the detailed specifications which will govern the concession should be stated and should become part of the concession contract.

The concession specifications should require that the commissionaire sell no commodities and employ no persons of which the school may disapprove. Standards of sanitation and methods of vending should also be explicitly stated. The contract should provide for payment of a percentage of gross receipts.

The flat-sum arrangement may work a hardship on the institution or the concessionaries. Net income should not be used as the basis for determining percentages as there is invariably the question of what costs the concessionaries will include in determining net proceeds. For interschool athletic events that draw considerable attendance, the management of the concessions becomes a business operation of such size that high schools and colleges have difficulty handling it effectively. In these instances most of the institutions have found it advantageous to have a concessionaries handle them. Experience has shown that more income has been received from a concessionaries than from a school-operated concession.

Increasing Gate Receipts—The best way to increase gate receipts from high school and college athletics is to have winning teams. However, there are other methods of making athletic contests more attractive to the public. A season ticket sold at a reduced rate is one of the most effective methods of increasing gate receipts. Such a plan guarantees a definite income despite poor teams and bad weather. It also provides funds early in the season when they are needed to get under way.

Adults are appreciative of the opportunity because it results in a saving to them. The price of a season ticket varies from 50 to 75 per cent of the total cost of tickets to each home game.

If season tickets are made transferable, they will prove more attractive to adults. In many communities reserved seats will appeal to certain adults. Some individuals are willing to pay more if they are assured of a good seat. There are always individuals who are unable to arrive at the game in time to get a good seat, who would not attend if reserved seats were not available. Well-coached teams appeal to the public. Public interest cools quickly when the players demonstrate poor fundamentals and appear disorganized. Many individuals will continue to support a team even in defeat if it gives the appearance of being well coached. In this connection, it is important to schedule opponents of approximately the same strength as the home team.

Unevenly matched teams are not good attractions. In addition to being well coached, teams will appeal more to spectators if they are smartly attired. One of the strongest attractions and most colourful features of athletic contests is the music, cheering, and pregame and half-time entertainment. Good officiating adds to everyone's enjoyment of a game. Attractive, accurate programs, a good scoreboard and a loudspeaker system with a capable announcer are all factors which provide satisfaction to the spectators. Other factors which contribute to the comfort and enjoyment of spectators are good seats, convenient entrances and exits, and a sufficient number of clean readily accessible restrooms. Good parking facilities near the athletic field or gymnasium is an important consideration. Contests should always be started at the time advertised. There is no question whatsoever that night football produces substantially more revenue than afternoon contests.

A large part of the adult public who find it impossible to leave their work or business in the afternoon are able to attend at night. There is, however, considerable opposition to night football from the standpoint of being less desirable for students. The importance of good publicity in increasing gate receipts is well established. The entire matter of publicity.

The Control of Finances

In the early days of interscholastic and intercollegiate athletics, the control of finances resided in the hands of the coach or graduate manager. These individuals were rarely called upon to account for the funds of the athletic department, and audits to check the athletic accounts were seldom used. Under these conditions, it is not surprising that a great deal of money was misused and misappropriated. Such financial practices naturally served to increase the evils of commercialization and subsidization.

High School

More financially and educationally sound methods of handling interscholastic athletic funds have evolved in recent years. In general, the trend is for these moneys to be handled in the same manner as other school funds. Adams, in an extensive study of interscholastic athletics, found that the persons responsible for the control of athletic funds in the order of frequency were: (1) the principal, (2) a member of the business department of the faculty, (3) the business manager of the school system, (4) the faculty manager of athletics, and (5) the superintendent.

The practice of having the treasurer or business manager of the board of education handle all athletic funds has much to recommend it. Such a plan centralizes all financial matters and insures more businesslike procedure. In particular, a more accurate audit is likely to result. However, many boards of education hesitate to assume the responsibility for athletic funds because they are not tax money and do not come within the scope of their duties. Adams data reveals that in the great majority of high schools all funds are handled within the school itself.

The recommended practice is to use a centralized accounting system whereby the responsibility for all financial accounts is centralized in one individual, such as the principal, commercial teacher, or other designated person. A system whereby the various accounts are decentralized and handled separately leads to confusion and inefficiency. In the centralized accounting system all athletic funds, along with all other activity funds, are deposited with the school treasurer.

Records are maintained for all deposits. When purchases are to be made, a purchase order in triplicate must be signed first by the athletic director and then certified by the school treasurer. One copy goes to the vendor, one copy is retained by the school treasurer, and the remaining copy is kept by the athletic director. Bills are not paid by the school treasurer until an invoice has been received from the vendor and checked by the athletic director or his representative that the materials received correspond with what has been ordered.

At periodic intervals, probably once a month, the

school treasurer submits a report to the athletic director and principal on the condition of the athletic budget. The school treasurer should be bonded for the largest amount of money that he will be responsible for during the year. His accounts should be audited annually by a qualified auditor.

Colleges and Universities

As the faculty assumed control of athletics, it undertook to remove the control of finances from the hands of those directly in charge of athletics. Although athletic directors still handle the funds in a number of institutions, the common practice today is to place the handling of athletic finances in the office of the general business manager of the college or university.

A number of the larger universities have a business manager within the department. The most satisfactory plan, however, is to have the university treasurer or the university business officer in actual charge of the care and distribution of athletic funds. This individual is usually a highly trained business man, well qualified to handle the funds of the athletic department. Under such a plan, the misuse of funds is reduced to a minimum. Under this plan, the director may make out a requisition for any purchases he desires to make.

This requisition is dent to the purchasing department, where two vouchers are made out and sent to the vendor. The vendor sends the equipment to the athletic department and returns the vouchers with the equipment as bill. The athletic department receives and checks the equipment and vouchers. One of the vouchers is kept on file and the other is sent to the business office, which the pays for the purchase

When the director desires cash, he makes out a requisition directly to the business office for the desired amount. Practically all institutions require receipts from the director or coach for his cash expenditures. The above plan has much to recommend it. The director may make purchases as he sees fit, as long as he remains within his budget.

He is not deprived of his authority to make expenditures. An unfortunate deprived of his authority to make expenditures. An unfortunate situation exists in some institutions where the business manager dominates the purchase of athletic equipment. If the director is unable to purchase wisely for his department, he is poorly qualified for his position. It would appear that his experience in this field and his knowledge of the specific use for which the purchases are intended should make it desirable that be at least consulted when purchases are made for his department.

Special Procedures in Large Cities

Interscholastic athletics in larger cities are usually co-ordinated by an individual who functions from a central office, usually the superintendent's office. Methods of operation vary from city to city. A common practice is to pool all gate receipts and to divide the total amount equally among all schools. In one city all athletic funds are turned over to the central office. Ten per cent of each athletic department's gross receipts is placed in a general funds. The remaining 90 per cent of income is available to each school to use as it desires. The money in the general fund is used to assist the poorer schools in financing their athletic programs.

In many cities the purchase of all athletic equipment is co-ordinated through the central office. This results in greater economy and, at the same time, insures each school a reasonable amount of equipment, with no school having an advantage over any other. A central organization is particularly desirable in those cities which have central stadiums and armories or coliseums. Oakland, Calif., provides an interesting example of centralized administration of interscholastic athletics.

In this city the school district assumes the responsibility of providing the coach and his salary, the supervisory staff, and all facilities including their maintenance. The gate receipts for all interscholastic athletic competition are deposited in a central fund. From this fund the director of physical education pays for all transportation costs, officiating, all medical expenses, including physician's fees, and all other expenses of a general nature. Each spring each school receives an identical allotment from the central fund. Schools are not permitted to use student body or other funds to supplement this allotment.

Each school is also provided with a petty cash fund of $25.00 each semester for incidental expenses. Athletic equipment is purchased on a centralized basis, although no school is required to purchase any item it does not want. On pieces of equipment which can be standardized, such as balls of all types, baseball bats, and shoulder pads, the coaches of the various sports reach an agreement as to what they prefer.

The specifications for these items are set up and bids invited. Samples equal or superior to the standard in quality, utility, and construction must be submitted. The coaches meet to make the final selection. All equipment not meeting the specifications is eliminated. The lowest bidder receives the order for equipment meeting the standards. In the matter of athletic clothing for the various sports each school decides upon the quality, pattern, and colours. Specifications are then set up and bids invited. Samples must be made available.

Again, the lowest bidder whose samples are satisfactory receives the order. When purchases are made the successful bidder is sent a purchase order. At the same time the school receives a duplicate purchase order. Upon receipt of the invoice from the seller and the duplicate purchase order from the school, properly signed and certifying that goods have been received in the quantity and quality as ordered, the bill is paid.

Synder enumerates the values of this equalization plan as follows:

1. It has lowered the cost of equipment because of competitive bidding.

2. It has permitted the less wealthy schools the use of other student body funds in about the same proportion per student as other schools.

3. It has provided an opportunity for school leaders to educate students on the basis outcomes of, and necessity for, equality of opportunity.

4. It has lowered each school to have adequate and safe transportation.

5. It has equalized standards and quality of equipment for all players.

6. It has eliminated special fund-raising events for purchase of equipment.

7. It has taken many of the burdens and time-consuming problems of athletics out of the hands of the coaches and department heads, thus permitting them more time for their physical education programs.

8. It has meant a real saving in that each school knowing approximately its athletic budget for each year, can plan wisely over a period of years for its acquisition of equipment.

Budget-Making

The first essential in the efficient management of any enterprise is to plan carefully in advance the income and the expenditures for a fiscal period. This process is essentially what is knowing as budget making. A budget is merely the complete financial plan, which is based upon the estimated expenditures to be made and the expected income. Budget making naturally originated in connection with business and governmental enterprises. The practice was found desirable and has since extended to most business enterprises and public service organizations, including the schools. The safest way to avoid deficits in physical education is to adopt budgets which limit the appropriations to the income and then confine the expenditures to the appropriations.

The budget results in planned spending. It is the best insurance of an equitable distribution of available funds to all the activities of the physical education department. Example of the spending of too much money on one sport resulting in the curtailment or elimination of other sports are not hard to find. The antagonism and embarrassment which may develop when this occurs could be eliminated if a budget were set up and followed. By means of the budget, the director can show where the money was spent and thus prevent any suspicion of misuse of funds.

The need for increased appropriations can be shown and justified more easily and effectively with a budget than without one. Extravagant and foolish buying will be checked, and comparisons with previous years and with other institutions can be made. The budget permits an analysis of the cost of the various sports and reveals where revision can be made, if necessary, with the least loss in the effectiveness of the department.

Procedure in Making a Budget

There are far more poorly constructed budgets than well-constructed ones, since few physical education departments construct them in accordance with the accepted principles of budgetary procedure. Every school presents an individual problem, but there are some fundamental principles which should be observed by any director who is constructing a budget. There is nothing mysterious about making one; nor is it necessary to be a business expert to do it. Any administrator can construct a satisfactory budget by following carefully a few fundamental principles. Physical education and athletic budgets are ordinarily prepared in March or April. They are made out annually.

The director of physical education has the responsibility for formulation the physical education budget. In colleges and universities the athletic director develops the athletic budget. This same situation prevails in the majority of high schools. However, the principal has this responsibility in many school. The superintendent, particularly in smaller schools, frequently carries this assignment. Other groups or individuals with this responsibility are the athletic council and the faculty manager of athletics.

The steps in constructing a budget are:

1. Collecting the necessary information.

2. Classifying the information.

3. Presenting and adopting the budget.

Collecting the Necessary Information

The information the budget maker collects is concerned with the expected income and necessary expenditures. In estimating the income for the coming fiscal period, the director must consider carefully all the sources from which he may expect revenue. He will know what guarantees will be received for all contests away from home unless the guarantee is dependent upon gate receipts. In the light of past years, how much can be expected at the gate for each home contest throughout the year?

Are there any factors during the coming year which will influence the gate receipts one way or another? Will the teams be particularly good or bad? Are colourful teams to be played? Are unusual attractions which will add to gate receipts to be provided? Are strong counter attractions occurring on the day of games? These are only a few of the questions which the director must consider as he estimates the anticipated revenue from gate receipts. He should be conservative in his estimates rather than optimistic. Weather conditions cannot be forecast for the coming year. Basketball is easier to estimate than football because weather conditions do not figure so heavily.

In regard to student fees, the director will need to consider any factors which may affect enrolment and the students' desire and ability to purchase season tickets. The appropriation from the board of education or the board of trustees can be estimated from previous appropriations. The director is usually familiar with the board's policies and will probably know whether any changes in the appropriation are likely. If revenue is anticipated from any additional sources, the amount may be calculated on the basis of previous income from these sources. The estimate of expenditures proceeds along similar lines.

The guarantees to be paid opponents are already known unless the gate receipts are to divided. The cost of transportation and other expenses of trips can be estimated quite accurately on the basis of previous trips. Approximately what will be the expense of each home game? Officials, student help, faculty help, policemen, publicity, tickets, and rent are some of the expense items to be considered in figuring the cost of home games. What purchases will have to be made? This is a difficult item to estimate. An inventory of the equipment on hand is necessary before any accurate estimate of future needs can be made. The cost of purchases may be secured fairly accurately by consulting the cost of the same items in the past. Investigation of the price other schools are paying is also of assistance. Price trends and the probable future prices must be considered. An average of the past five years may be used to estimate the cost of other items, such as laundry, medical attention and supplies, scouting, awards, intramural activities, and equipment repairs. Office supplies, insurance, telephone, and telegraph expense can be estimated on the basis of previous years' expenditures. The director should never forget that the budget is no better than the time spent estimating it. Information about these various items should be gathered and complied continuously.

All the needs observed should be noted throughout the year. The entire department should be encouraged to inform the director of present and future needs in order that he may know where new expenditures are needed most. The director should not fail to consult the various staff members who are in a position to assist in supplying needed information. He should keep in constant touch with the supply houses and read current catalogues on the cost of physical education and athletic equipment.

Some administrators resort to the practice of "padding" the budget on the assumption that the persons who finally approve it will make a reduction anyway. By including expenditures which are not really necessary or by overestimating the cost of certain items, these administrators hope to build up a cushion which will enable them to obtain the funds they actually consider necessary. Such a practice is dishonest and , in the long run, reflects adversely against the administrator. It breeds distrust and engenders suspicion. Administrators should present honest budgets and be prepared to justify them.

Classifying the Information

After the information has been gathered it should be classified. This insures uniformity of presentation and makes for accuracy in planning. It facilitates the gathering and compiling of the data, and it makes easier the reviewing and revising of the estimates. The form the classification takes should resemble the form of the final budget. The information relating to capital outlays and maintenance and operation of the plant is not included in the physical education budget. In high school and most college budgets salaries are not included. All the information is classified under two general heads: one dealing with the information concerning revenue and the other bearing on expenditures. Every item for which an expenditure is contemplated, even though it may amount to only a few dollars, should be reflected in the budget.

These smaller items can be segregated under larger headings, but the detailed information should be available if requested. Sample classifications for physical education and athletic budgets.

Presenting and Adopting the Budget

In colleges the physical education budget is first approved by the athletic committee or board, which usually administers the policies of the department. If no such group exists, the president probably approves it. Final approval of the budget is usually made by the board of trustees or board of regents. High school budgets are first approved by the principal, then by the superintendent, and, finally, by the board of education. At times, the business manager of the college or high school approves the budget before it goes to the board of education or board of trustees. The budget should be adopted before any purchases are made or expenditures entered into for the next year. The fiscal period in use is frequently a factor in the success or shortcomings of the budget, and for this reason, it seems advisable to suggest July 1st as the first day of the fiscal year, because the latter will then approximately coincide with the school year.

Administering the Budget

After the physical education budget is adopted, it becomes the financial program of the department. After its adoption, should it be followed rigidly? There are some who believe that after the budget has been adopted the expenditures should be made as directed. Others hold to the view that the budget should be reviewed again when the expenditures are actually to be made. The general practice, however, is to follow the budget figures fairly closely.

The variation is usually from 3 to 5 per cent in which the expenditures exceed or fail to match the appropriations. Practically all budgets make provisions for readjustments. Emergencies are certain to occur, and the budget should be elastic enough to provide for them. There are several different plans which may be followed. An emergency or contingency fund may be set aside in the original budget. But if this fund is too small, the administrator may feel cramped in his efforts to adjust appropriations to unforeseen circumstances. If on the other hand, the fund is too large, it may encourage waste and carelessness and thus defeat one of the main purposes of budget making. The most common plan is to transfer funds from one budgetary item which appears likely not to need all the available money to the item on which the demand has unexpectedly increased.

Such transfers, if appreciable, however, must have the approval of the athletic board, the business manager, or perhaps, in college, the president. Proper records should be kept in order that the actual revenue and expenditures may be compared with the budget estimates. These records are invaluable to the administrator as he prepares his new budget. In addition, they are of value in making necessary adjustments where indicated in the current budget. The administrator should receive monthly reports so that he may know the relationship of income of expenses with the budget estimates. He needs to know whether actual income is in line with his estimates. Insofar as expenditures are concerned he must always know the amount appropriated, the amount expended, commitments which must be paid but have not yet been received, and the unallocated balance. If income is much lower than anticipated during the first half of the fiscal period, it might be indicated that expenditures should be reduced in the second half of the period to prevent a serious deficit.

In those institutions where salaries are paid from athletic revenue, a salaries account should be carried. This would include all salaries which are not paid directly by the institution. The preceding classification is used as follows: every expenditure made is allocated to some activity. Thus, if a telephone bill for football is paid, football is charged with the amount of the bill.

The Accounting Procedure

The proper functioning of the budget and the success of budgetary procedures depend largely upon an adequate accounting system. Although the director is rarely in charge of the accounting procedure, he should have some conception of it. It would be impossible of the director to conduct his department on a businesslike basis without the help of the accounting system. It serves to restrict the expenditures to income. Unanticipated tendencies in cost and income will be revealed in time to revise the budget. The director secures much of the information for drafting the budget from the accounting records.

The accounting method protects the director or the coach from charges of carelessness and misuse of funds. Upon the information supplied by the accounting records, the director can base his request for further financial assistance from the board. The individual in charge of the physical education finances is interested in current income and expenses. The accounting method classifies revenue on the receipts side of the budget. However, the recording of current expenditures is more complex. Pittenger states that there are four essential parts in recording expenditures.

- Original records of every transaction involving expenditure of funds are preserved. These records are almost indispensable when the time comes to audit the physical education accounts.

- Some from of day book or journal record of expenditures is often useful to serve, on the one hand, as a guide to the original record files, and on the other, as the basis from which to post the regular ledger accounts. This feature is omitted, however, in the smaller high schools, where the ledger pages are posted directly from the original records of financial transactions.

- The heart of the system is the classified ledger record in which the completed expenditures are regularly posted against the budgetary appropriations in order to reveal the amount expended and the amount remaining for each and every budgetary item at any time.

- The final state of the accounting procedure is

reached in the periodical reports, balances sheet, and revenue statement from the accounting officer to the director of physical education setting forth the current financial situation.

Petty Cash Fund

It is an established business procedure for the administrator to have a small petty cash fund of approximately $25.00 from which he can make small purchase. It is much simpler to make purchases of less than two dollars directly rather than to make out a purchase requisition. Receipts for all purchases should be obtained. When the petty cash fund is exhausted, the receipts should be submitted along with the request for an additional appropriation.

The Annual Audit

Provision for frequent, regular audits must be made if the budget is to function properly as an instrument of fiscal control. An audit serves as a check on the manner in which the director administers the budget and gives assurance that the budgetary provisions are being carried out. The audit should be made by competent auditors who are not directly connected with the administration of the school funds. The great majority of school follow this practice. The head of the commercial department often makes the audit. The audit should be made annually, because the work involved is less confusing and a closer check can be made than when it is delayed. Good budgetary procedure requires an external, independent, annual audit.

Handling School Funds

School are frequently careless in their management

of gate receipts. The large sums of money which often are involved should call forth all precautions to insure against loss. Another argument for the sale of tickets in advance of the game is that it prevents the accumulation of large sums of money. Theft insurance is carried by all large schools, and the game manager is usually bonded. Plenty of police protection should be provided, particularly when the funds are collected and taken from the ticket offices Unless the amount is very small, arrangements should be made to deposit the gate receipts in a bank or police station after the game.

It is a cardinal principal in schools as well as in business organizations that all financial transactions should be recorded in some tangible way. It is for this reason that receipts for all purchases are necessary. By the same token, when money is received receipts should be given and carbons retained. Such receipts are essential when the accounts are audited. An accurate record must also be available of ticket sales at athletic contest. Ordinarily this is done by recording the number on the roll prior to and following the game. These data are also necessary for the auditors.

Expense Reports

Following a trip by a school athletic team a report should be made of the expenses which were incurred. Receipts should be obtained for all expenditures for which cash is paid. Most of the University of Pennsylvania. The use of such a form facilitates the accounting of the expenses and is a more businesslike procedure than that followed in school which do not use any forms.

Game Reports

In many schools the athletic director is expected to provide game reports after each contest. This report includes such items as attendance, gate receipts, complimentary tickets, expenses, other income, weather conditions, and the score. These reports serve as a valuable record for future use, especially in the preparation of future budgets.

Interschool Financial Agreement

Practically all colleges and large high school sign contracts with each other for all interschool contests. The practice of making verbal financial agreements still persists in some of the smaller high schools. Such a procedure is hardly businesslike, and it naturally lends itself to misunderstanding and mistakes. In order to make financial agreements between schools more understandable, more explicit, and more binding, regular contracts should be signed by both schools for all contests. These contract forms are supplied by the state associations or conferences.

6

The Organizations of Physical Education

Historical Background

In the eleventh century a great movement toward associations began to sweep over the cities of Europe. These associations were formed around numerous aspects of social life. By the end of the fifteenth century this spirit of organization had become prominent among many classes of city dwellers. The legal, medical, and teaching professions were among those banded together at that. Since that time many of the profession have become better organized and new ones have been established in Europe and on other continents.

The American Association for Health, Physical Education, And Recreation

The American Association for Health and Physical Education was founded officially in November, 1885. At that time Doctor William G. Anderson of Adelphi

Academy, Brooklyn, later physical director at Yale University, was instrumental in calling together a group of about sixty teachers for the purpose of organizing a society of physical education. The gathering resulted in the formation of the American Association for the Advancement of Physical Education, with Dr. Edward Hitchcock of Amherst College, as the first president.

The objectives of the association were stated as follows: "To disseminate knowledge concerning physical education, to improve methods, and by meetings of the members to bring those interested in the subject in closer relation to each other. The new association was particularly fortunate in obtaining prominent leaders in the early history of physical education for its presidents. Among them were Dr. Hitchcock of Amherst, Dr. Sargent of Harvard, Dr. Gulick of the Y.M.C.A., Dr. Arnold. There have been several constitutions in the history of the society, and amendments to them have not been uncommon. Each new one was created in response to new problems presented by the rapid growth of the organization and the necessity of providing adequate representation for all sections of the country and all the specialized interests within the profession. In the third constitution, adopted in 1903, the name of the organization was changed to the American Physical Education Association. This remained the official name until June, 1937, When it became The American Association for Health and physical Education-A Department of the N.E.A. In 1938, "Recreation" was added to this title. This department of the N.E.A. now includes five divisions: Health Education Division, Physical Education Division, Recreation Division, General Division, and Men's Athletics Division. In addition, the board of directors of the AAHPER has approved in principle a tentative divisional structure for girls' and women's sports.

The present National Section for Girls' and Women's Sports may serve as a tentative division through the 1958 AAHPER convention, after which it may be evaluated by the board of directors and thus become the sixth division. There are now four divisional Vice-president; one each for Health Education, Physical Education, Recreation, and Men's Athletics.

General Organization

The general structure of this organization may be summarized as follows:

Board of Directors—The board of directors consists of the president, the president-elect, the immediate past-president, the vice-presidents, one representative from each of the six districts, and the executive secretary-treasurer. The roster of the board is published in each issue of The Journal of Health-Physical Education Recreation.

Representative Assembly—The representative assembly consists of the board of directors, the district presidents, and twelve representatives from each division as designated by division codes. The representative assembly also includes additional state representatives, based on number of regular, professional, and life members in the AAHPER as follows: one representative for 25 to 100 members; two representative for 101 to 300 members; three representatives for 301 to 500 members; and one additional representative for each 250 additional members above 500. State associations with less than 25 members may petition the executive secretary for representation in the representative assembly.

The executive secretary-treasurer is also a nonvoting member. The representative assembly among other duties effects all changes in the constitution and bylaws, initiates such business as it deems desirable, and exercises veto power over all action taken by the board of directors upon a three-fourths vote of all present at official meetings or by a three-fourths majority of the total membership by mail vote.

Committees

There are four kinds of committees-standing, president's continuing, and joint committees. All but the standing committees are indefinite in number and are appointed for relatively specific duties.

Among the standing committees are committees on facilities, finance, international relations, honour awards, necrology, resolution, membership, and vocational guidance.

Organization by Interests

There are five division, each comprising several sections, responsible for convention program planning within their respective fields and for various specialized committee and publication projects. Each division elects a chairman, as does each section within each division. The division and sections are:

1. Physical Education Division

(a) Elementary School Physical Education

(b) Secondary School Physical Education

(c) College Physical Education

2. Health Education Division

(a) School and College Health Services

(b) College Health Education

(c) Dental health Education

(d) School Lunch

(e) Elementary School Health Education

(f) Community Health Education

(g) Safety Education Section

(h) Secondary School Health Education

3. Men's Athletics Division

(a) Sports Officiating

(b) Winter Sports

(c) Spring Sports

(d) Athletic Administration

(e) Fall Sports Section

(f) Athletic Training Section

(g) Intramural Athletics

4. General Division

(a) Dance

(b) Student

(c) Therapeutic

(d) Research Council

(e) Research

(f) Professional and Public Relations

(g) Professional Education

(h) Measurement and Evaluation

(i) International Relations

(j) Council on Equipment and Supplies

(k) Camping and Outdoor Education

(l) Athletics—Girls and Women

(m) Aquatics

(n) Administration and Supervision

5. Recreation Division

(a) Voluntary and Youth Sewing Agencies

(b) Recreational Therapy

(c) Recreation in Religious Organizations

(d) Public Recreation

(e) Industrial Recreation

Affiliated Organizations

The following associations are affiliated with the

AAHPER:

1. Society of State Directors of Health, Physical Education, and Recreation

2. Physical Education Society of the Y.M.C.A.' of North America

3. Phi Epsilon Kappa

4. Phi Delta Pi

5. National Committee for Health and Physical Education of the National Association of Jewish Centre Workers

6. National Collegiate Athletic Association

7. National Board of Y.W.C.A. of the United States

8. National Association for Physical Education of College Women

9. National Association for Intercollegiate Athletics

10. Delth Psi Kappa

11. College Physical Education Association

12. Canadian AHPER

13. Boys' Clubs of America, Inc.

14. Association for Physical and Mental Rehabilitation

15. American Youth Hostels, Inc.

16. American Academy of Physical Education

17. American School Health Association

Geographical Organization

Forty-eight state associations and the District of

Columbia are grouped into six districts, which hold annual conventions and elect district president who serve as members of the representative assembly. The districts and the sovereign units included in each are:

1. Northwest District—Idaho, Montana, Oregon, Washington,

2. Southwest District—Arizona, California, Nevada, New Mexico, Utah.

3. Southern District—Alabama, Arkansas, Florida, Georgia, Kentucky, Louisiana, Mississippi, North Carolina, Oklahoma, South Carolina, Tennessee, Taxas, Virginia.

4. Midwest District—Illinois, Indiana, Michigan, Ohio, West Virginia, Wisconsin.

5. Eastern District—Connecticut, Delaware, District of Columbia, Maine, Maryland, Massachusetts, New Hampshire, New Jersey, New York, Pennsylvania, Rhode Island, Vermont.

6. Central District—Colorado, Iowa, Kansas, Minnesota, Missouri, Nebraska, North Dakota, South Dakota, Wyoming.

Publications

The American Physical Education Review, for over thirty years the official organ of the association, was founded in 1896. Previous to that time ten reports had been issued each year. The review, unlike the reports, aimed to do more than publish the papers of the convention. In 1922 the Review published ten issues a year and gradually expanded in size. Its contributors included many figures well known in educational and scientific research. In 1930 the name of the official publication was changed to the Journal of Health and Physical Education. The present title is Journal of Health-Physical Education-Recreation. It is published monthly September to April inclusive, and biomonthly in Many and June. The content of the Journal deals predominantly with practical, popular material written so that the layman can understand it. Regular membership costs $5.00 and carries with it subscription to the journal. The association also publishes a Research Quarterly, containing four regular issues per year, in March, May, October, and December. Besides the regular issues, occasional supplements are published.

The Research Quarterly is sent to professional, sustaining, and honorary members, and patrons without charge. As the name implies, the Quarterly deals with research, scientific, and summary material of a more technical nature and serves as stimulus for more scholarly work in the profession.

In addition to the two regular magazines the association now publishes considerable other material in book, magazine, and report forms.

Additional Organizations

A brief presentation of information concerning a number of other physical education and semi-physical education organizations is included to illustrate the types and variety of forms these organizations take in the United States.

National Section for Girls' and Women's Sports

The National Section for Girls' and Women's Sports, frequently referred to as the NSGWS, is one of the largest, most active and influential sections of the American Association for health, Physical Education, and Recreation. It is the only organization in the country which is concerned with the total sports program for girls and women from junior high school age and up. The membership includes all women members of the AAHPER who are interested in sports for girls and women. These women are trained leaders and teachers in high schools, colleges, and universities, business, recreation, industrial plants, military services, and private and public clubs and agencies.

The purpose of the section is to promote wholesome sports programs for all girls and women. At all times the welfare of the player is of prime concern. The purpose is achieved by :

Formulating and publishing guiding principles and standards for the administrator, leader, official, and player.

Publishing and interpreting rules governing sports for girls and women.

Disseminating accurate information on the conduct of girls' and women's sports.

Stimulating and evaluating research in the field of girls' and women's sports.

NSGWS is a continuous working section, with an intricate constitutionalized national organization and many specific annual commitments. Its business is transacted by a legislative board made up of officers, district representatives, standing committee chairman, and advisory members. Some of the commitments which members of the board assume annually are the editing and publishing of the sports guides and similar publications, promotion of women officials for sports played by girls and women, planning of programs for demonstrations, clinics and meetings at local, state, and district levels, and the promotion at the national level of all its services.

There are eleven standing committees: audiovisual, finance, international relations, nominations and elections, operating code, public relations, publications, research, rules and editorial, standards, and women's official rating. The rules and editorial committee is made up of the chairmen of the eighteen sports committees which publish at regular intervals guides for aquatics, winter sports, and outing activities; archery-riding; basketball; bowling-fencing-golf; field hockey-lacrosse; recreational games-volleyball; softball-track and field; soccer-speedball; and tennis-badminton. These publications include articles pertinent to the various sports and the official rules for girls' and women's sports.

Since the merger of the NSGWS with the Women's Division of the National Amateur Athletic Federation, the NSGWS has become the authoritative body in establishing standards for girls' and women's sports. Statements on standards prepared by its Standards Committee were first published in 1937. To insure their continued usefulness and to make them applicable with present needs, trends, and practices, the statements on standards have been constantly reviewed and revised.

They have been accepted widely by professional schools of physical education, physical educators throughout the country, recreation groups, and the military services. In 1941 an adaptation of the standards was published under the title of Desirable Practices in

Sports for Girls and Women. In 1948, specific standards were published for each of the team, dual, and individual sports.

The unique of this organization is the number of women who give generously of their time and effort because of their interest in sports for girls and women and because of their firm belief in the principles and standards of the NSGWS. Through this voluntary participation the members of the NSGWS render a vital service to youth as well as to the profession and, at the same time, have opportunities for their own professional growth.

The American Academy of Physical Education

Luther H. Gulick was largely responsible for organizing the American Academy of Physical Education in 1904—05. This body continued until World War I. The academy was revived in 1926. It was officially founded and a constitution was adopted in 1930 with twenty-nine charter members. The general purposes of the American Academy of Physical Education are to advance knowledge and common understanding, to raise standards, and to bestow honours in physical education and in related areas. More specific purposes are (a) to elect as fellows persons who have made significant professional contributions; (b) to stimulate needed research through guidance and advice; (c) to disseminate professional information both within this country and in foreign lands; (d) to assist with the enactment of appropriate legal measures in local, state, and federal governments; (e) to encourage competent persons to enter the profession; and (f) to recognize meritorious and scholarly achievements by indicative awards and citations.

Membership consists of (a) active fellows, (b) associate fellows, (c) corresponding fellows, (d) fellows in memoriam, (e) honorary fellows in memoriam, and (f) fellows retired. Voting privileges and holding office are restricted to active fellows, who alone pay the initiation fee of $10.00 and annual dues of $10.00. Selection of all fellows in made by the membership committee with election by active fellows of the academy. A two-thirds majority of all votes cast is required for election to membership. Publications include papers and reports presented at annual meetings. As is true of most significant organizations in the field, committees are used to assist in expediting the work of the academy. These are of two types; standing committees, of which there are four; and presidents' committees, of which are currently three.

The College Physical Education Association. In 1897 nine prominent physical educators met in New York and established the ground work for the organization of the Society of College Gymnasium Directors. Dr. J. W. Seaver was elected president, and Dr. W. L. Savage was elected secretary-treasurer. In 1909 the name of the organization was changed to the Society of College Directors of Physical Education, which, in 1933, was changed to the present one, the College Physical Education Association.

In contrast to the former tendency to restrict membership both as to type and position, the present tendency seems to favour expansion and extension of the benefits of the organization to all who are interested. Many of the leading administrators of physical education in colleges are or have been members of this society. Several major projects have been undertaken by the society, the first of which was to perfect strength tests for college men. Other projects include standardization of terms in physical education; improvement of physical education buildings and plants; conduction of curriculum research; improvement of the administration of intercollegiate athletics and of the sanitation of swimming pools; presenting proposed relationship of college physical education to national preparedness; dealing with various subjects of a timely nature, such as proposal of policies concerning accepting military training for physical education and hygiene credit; accepting joint sponsorship with the AAHPER and the national Association for Physical Education of College Women of two national conferences; and sponsoring of graduate studies which appear important to the profession.

There are three types of membership; active for active college teachers or administrators in the field, associate for active members in related fields, and honorary.

The National Association of Intercollegiate Athletics: The NAIA believes in the socializing values of intersectional and national competition. Originally named the National Association of Intercollegiate Basketball at its inception in 1940, this association changed its name in 1952 to the National Association of Intercollegiate Athletics. It now has well over 400 member schools, which are divided into 32 districts, each of which is entitled to qualify a team to represent its district member institutions at national tournaments and meets. At the present time national championship plans are set up for crosscountry, football, basketball, track and field, golf, and tennis.

The tentative aims and objectives which are now in

the process of being voted upon for approval by the member schools, and may well be established by the time this book goes to press, consider among other goals: that the individual be developed to the fullest extent; that the entire program be evaluated in terms of educational purposes; that inclusion of prescribed courses, intramural, and extramural activities, and intercollegiate athletics all be included in the broadly based program of physical education; that intercollegiate athletics has the same general aims as the rest of the program but officers additional educational experiences; that the intercollegiate athletic program in all of its phases stress moral and ethical values; that the intercollegiate athletic program should be controlled completely by the college administration; that the broadly based physical education department should have a place in the structure and function of the educational institution as do other departments; that members should compete with others having the same standards and practices; that students competing in intercollegiate athletics be bona fide students whose financial aid, except that form home, be administered by the college; and that the association and member school work co-operatively to improve programs of intercollegiate athletics.

The American College of Sports Medicine

The sports medicine movement in Europe dates from the late 1920's. There are bibliographies in German and Italian that publish material that goes back as far as 1920. In south America the Sports medicine Association of Argentina held a celebration of its twentieth birthday in April, 1955.

In the United States there has been much activity in

one area of sports medicine for many years, the area of the prevention and treatment of sports injuries; but the broader fields was not entered in this country until the American College of Sports Medicine was organized at the New York meeting of the American Association of Health, Physical Education, and Recreation on September.

In the sports medicine organizations of Europe and Southern America, sports is defined very broadly, and the term is applied not only to competitive athletics but to almost the whole field of physical education activities, including exercise therapy in hospitals, convalescent centres, rehabilitation centres, and all exercise-type activities designed to serve the human race.

The term medicine is likewise very broadly conceived and embraces not only physicians but exponents of numerous biological sciences that are interested in improving the welfare of mankind. Among the medical fraternity who have become interested in sports medicine and who have contributed to its literature may be listed (1) internists, (2) cardiologists, (3) physiatrists, (4) psychiatrists, (5) orthopedists, (6) practitioners of general surgery, (7) those who are frequently classed as "team physicians."

Among the scientists who may or may not be graduates of schools of medicine may be listed (1) pathologists, (2) physiologists, (3) chemists, especially biochemists, (4) specialists in nutrition, (5) geneticists or eugenists interested in problems of the heredity of qualities or eugenists interested in problems of the heredity of qualities making for success in sports, (6) anatomists and muscle-kinesiologists, (7) anthropologists and anthropometrists, (8) psychologists, and (9) hygienists.

In addition, there are the large groups of (1) physical educators, (2) athletic coaches, (3) exercise therapists, (4) mechanics-kinesiologists, (5) athletics trainers, (6) health educators, (7) recreation specialists, and (8) general educators and educators and education administrators.

There are many interdiscipline problems, of which hundreds could be cited. For example, there are (1) problems of sports medicine that interest the coaches and the intuitionists; (2) those that interest coaches, the trainers, and physiatrists; (3) those with which the physiologists and pathologists are concerned; (4) the growth problems that interest both the educators and the anthropologists; (5) the problems of technique that interest the coaches, the physical of mechanical analysis of motor skills; and (6) problems of girls and women's sports that interest the gynaecologists, the psychologists and physiologists, and the educational administrators, as well as the physical educators.

The above-mentioned fields of medicine, of physical education, and of science function through research laboratories of many types, through schools and colleges, sports clubs, recreation facilities, private organization, hospitals, convalescent and rehabilitation centres, and many other groups. The areas involved include labour and industry, agriculture, all branches of the armed services, social centres, athletic administrative organizations in this country, such as the NCAA, the AAU, the Olympic committees, and numerous other public, private, and semiprivate organizations.

Among the areas served are those of the physiology of exercise, applied anatomy and kinesiology, applied anthropology, some fields of hygiene, the pathologies related to sports, clinical sports medicine, physical medicine generally, surgery and orthopedics applied to sports injuries, exercise therapy, the psychology of sports, special problems in sports of girls and women, the techniques of training, the pedagogy of sports, the functions of the trainer, and research in these various areas as applied to sports and physical education generally.

The American College of Sports Medicine meets annually and, whenever possible, with the American Association for Health, Physical Education, and Recreation at its national meeting. The organization has a president; three vice-presidents—one for medicine, one for physiology, and one for physical education; a secretary; and a treasurer. There are ten members of its administrative council, and a total of twenty members of the board of trustees, including the officers and members of the administrative council. As of the date of publication of this text, there are ten functioning committees.

In the European associations—international and national—practically all of the active members are physicians. In South America and the United States there are many physical educators, physiologists, and other scientists enrolled as regular members or "fellows," as they are termed in the American College of Sports Medicine.

This field, which in the United States is a new one, bids fair to develop rapidly and to make an increasing contribution to co-operative research in the field of sports, through the working together of physicians, physiologists, anatomists, pathologists, nutritionists, physical educators, and others interested in the area of sports and physical education.

National Association for Physical Education of College Women

The purpose of this association is to study problems relating to the physical education of college women to the end of increasing its effectiveness. There are five district associations: the Eastern Association for Physical Education of College Women, Southern Association for Physical Education of College Women, Midwest Association for Physical Education of College Women, Central Association for Physical Education of College Women, and Western Society for Physical Education of College Women. The Eastern Association was the parent organization, and Miss Amy Homans was chiefly responsible for its organization.

The first preliminary meeting was held, upon her invitation, at Wellesley College in 1910. Similar meetings were held for the next few years, but the Association of Directors of Physical Education for Women was no organized until 1915. In 1916 the constitution was adopted.

At the present time the association maintains a rather extensive committee structure which promotes studies in various areas. There are standing committees on constitution, research and studies, public relations, international relations, honorary memberships, legislation, and an editorial committee. There are, in addition, special committees on historical records, professional leadership, intramural and extramural sports and dance, and the instructional program for college women. Meetings of the association are held biennially. These meetings alternate between short meetings and longer workshop meetings of a week in length.

The Society of State Directors of Health, Physical Education, and Recreation

This society, affiliated with the American Association for Health, Physical Education, and Recreation was organized in 1926, with Carl L. Sharader as its first president. The practice of employing state chiefs, consultants, co-ordinators, and directors is comparatively recent. There were but four in 1918, nineteen in 1936, and thirty-six in 1947. Additional physical education legislation and the development of more state physical education syllabi point toward the installation of more state physical education syllabi point toward the installation of more state directors of physical education. There are active and associate members; the former consists of directors and the latter their professional assistants.

Official titles of those in charge of the state departments of health, physical education, and recreation vary. In some cases the director is in charge of health and not of physical education.

The Young Men's Christian Association

In 1841 George Williams, and Englishman, started the movement that developed into the Y.M.C.A. in 1844. The purpose was almost entirely religious. This movement spread to other countries, including the United States, where the first American Y.M.C.A. was formed in 1851 at Boston. Little or no consideration was given to physical education until 1856, when the National Convention proposed establishing gymnasiums. This proposal met with approval, and, in a few years, provisions were made in some of the buildings for physical activities. This aspect has developed until practically all branches today provide for a number of phases of physical education.

There was a scarcity of qualified men to serve as physical directors in the early days, and it became necessary to train men of sound character who could do this work. One of the first Christian physical directors was Robert J. Roberts of Boston, who did much in the way of volunteer leadership to expand his own program. His leaders' clubs provided young men who were employed by other associations as professionals.

In 1885 the Springfield Y.M.C.A. College in Springfield, Mass., established a department of physical education that was headed by Luther Halsey Gulick, the first secretary for physical education on the Y.M.C.A. National Council Staff, and he employed, Robert J. Roberts as one of his instructors. Gulick continued his dual role in the organization until 1901.

In 1890, what is now George Williams College was founded in Chicago and carried on summer work on Lake Geneva in Wisconsin for the training of physical education secretaries and those responsible for other phases or work.

Leadership at these training schools was provided by men who were influential not only in the Y.M.C.A. but in physical education and medical circles outside the association. Dr. James H. Mc Curdy succeeded Dr. Gulick at springfield College and served until the late thirties, when George Affleck became active head of the department. Following World War II. Arthur A. Esslinger gave leadership to the physical education department at Springfield College, and he, in turn, was succeeded by Ellis H. Champlin.

Leadership at George Williams College was provided by D. Henry F. Kallenberg, who was succeeded by Martin I. Foos. He was Followed by Charles G. Giauque, and then Arthur H. Steinhaus was named director.

The world-wide games of basketball and volleyball were both developed through Y.M.C.A. initiative. Basketball was devised in 1891 by James Naismith at Springfield College, and Volleyball by William Morgan, a Y.M.C.A. physical director at Holyoke, Mass.

In 1896 the Athletic League of the Y.M.C.A.'s of North America was formed. This provided the organization for formal competition within the Y.M.C.A. and helped weld the association into an operating unit.

In 1901 the magazine, Physical Training, was started by Dr. Gulick, and, in 1903, when the Physical Directors' Society of North America was organized, the society assumed responsibility for this publication. In 1927 the name of the publication was changed to Journal of Physical Education, and it continues to the present time under this title.

In 1923, when the former Y.M.C.A. organization was reformed and the National Council of the Y.M.C.A.'s of the United States was organized, the executive committee of the Athletic League of the Y.M.C.A.'s of North America was used as the basis for the National Y.M.C.A. Physical Education Committee, Commissioned by the National Board of the National Council.

Leadership for the national work as noted earlier was provided by Dr. Gulick. The position was filled from 1906 to 1919 by Dr. George J. Fisher. Dr. John Brown, Jr. carried the responsibilities for twenty years, to 1939, when he was shifted to another assignment and then retired the next year. In May, 1943, Dr. Harold T. Friermood, formerly physical director at Dayton, Ohio, Y.M.C.A. was named to the national post, and he continues to the present time.

A group of European Y.M.C.A. physical directors who had studied at the extension department of Springfield College set up in Geneva, Switzerland, conceived the idea of a World Basketball Federation in the late twenties or early thirties. This was formed with a modest beginning and grew rapidly. Through this organization it was possible to have basketball included in the Olympic Games in 1936, and, at the present time, some seventy countries of the world are members of the World Basketball Federation.

In 1947 the World Volleyball Federation was established in Paris, and the United States had two official delegates to the organization meeting. The initial membership of twelve charter nations has now grown to sixty countries, and volleyball was included for the first time in the Pan-American Games in Mexico city in 1955.

Throughout the Y.M.C.A. emphasis has been placed upon health and fitness since the early days. The value of play, relaxation, constructive recreation, and adequate physical activity have always characterized Y.M.C.A. programs. The first Y.M.C.A. swimming and operates some 700 indoor pools and carries on aquatic programs in some 700 resident camps.

With the emphasis upon coeducational activities and family education, an increasing number of women and girl members has been recorded each year until, at this writing, 17 per cent of the more than three million Y.M.C.A. membership consists of women and girls.

The Physical Education Department of the Y.M.C.A. aims to develop physical mental, and moral efficiency in its members by means of exercise, recreation, and education on a group as well as on an individual basis.

The purpose of the Young Men's Christian Association continues through the years as seeking to develop Christian personality and a Christian society, and it has utilized these principles and this fellowship for the benefit of all.

The Young Women's Christian Association

The Young Women's Christian Association originated in England about 1860. At that time the purpose was almost entirely religious. The first Y.W.C.A. in America was established in Boston in 1866 under the leadership of Mrs. Henry Durant; but not until 1877 was any significant attempt made to introduce physical education as a phase of the work of the organization.

The introduction took the form of a calisthenics class, which was soon copied by other nearby associations. To this type of activity was added games and recreational activities.

This aspect of the work proved interesting and progressed rapidly. In 1884 one floor of the new building in Boston was given over to Durant Gymnasium, and Miss Anna Wood, from the Wellesley College faculty, was secured to direct the activities of this first Y.W.C.A.

gymnasium. By 1890 physical education work was closely identified with the Y.W.C.A. Many buildings were provided with gymnasiums.

The fourfold aim of the Boston Y.W.C.A. at this time, which stressed the elevation of women physically, mentally, morally, and spiritually, was generally accepted by other associations. The physical education program aimed to provide for the young women not in college what the college program provided for those who were there.

7

The Purchase and Maintenance of Equipments

The purchase and care of equipment was not an important responsibility for those in charge of the first interschool teams, for the players furnished their own equipment. As interscholastic and intercollegiate athletics grew, schools undertook to equip the players. For a number of years the equipment item did not assume large proportions because little equipment was needed.

The athletic program was limited to a few sports, the squads were small, and the players were not equipped so elaborately and completely as they are today. Furthermore, the cost of athletic equipment was considerably less than it is at present. Today, the purchase and care of equipment constitutes one of the director's most important responsibilities. Most athletic departments feel obligated to protect the members of the teams to a reasonable extent with adequate equipment.

Not only are the injuries reduced but well-equipped, well-dressed teams appeal more to the public than unattractive teams. Equipment expense has become one of the largest items in the athletic budget and a great deal of money may be wasted unless equipment is purchased carefully and cared for properly.

A great deal has been learned about buying and caring for equipment in recent years. Directors have purchased equipment more wisely and have cared for it more carefully since the beginning of World War II. Many of the expense items in the budget do not lend themselves readily to reductions, but directors have found numerous ways by which they can reduce the expense of equipment without appreciably impairing its effectiveness and appearance. It is essential that every director know equipment thoroughly and be acquainted with the policies, methods, and techniques by which equipment might be bought and cared for most economically.

Provision of Equipment by School

Practically all schools provide the playing equipment for the service and intramural programs. The student is expected to furnish his own uniform. Many schools provide towels and towel service at no cost to students, but many make a charge for this service. In still other schools the provision of clean towels is the responsibility of the student. This means that he must bring his own towel and take it home for laundering.

This practice is not recommended because of the problems involved in administering it. For interschool athletics it is highly desirable to have the school to furnish most items of equipment, including uniforms.

Adams study revealed that in 60 per cent of large high schools, 48 per cent of medium-sized high schools, and 34 per cent small high schools, all personal equipment was furnished to squad members. In approximately 62 per cent of the small high schools and 45 per cent of the medium-sized high schools, shoes were not furnished by the school. Many high schools rent shoes—particularly football shoes—to the players. An appreciable percentage or gloves. Virtually all schools provide playing uniforms, but it is exceptional for a school to furnish such specialized and personal equipment as golf clubs and tennis rackets.

Students should not be required to provide all or part of their uniform, because, inevitably, some will be unable to afford to become candidates for teams. Equally undesirable is the practice of using cheap, ill-fitting equipment which has been borrowed or handed down year after year. Some parents will purchase football shoes which are too large with the hope that they will last the student three years. The provision of most items of athletic equipment by the school is a standard toward which all physical education departments should work.

Purchasing Policies

After the need have been determined the director is prepared to buy. But the purchase of athletic equipment involved much more than merely buying goods to the limit of the budget. Every director is anxious to obtain the best service and the longest life in equipment per dollar spent. In order to attain this objective there are some recognized policies of buying which might be followed. Purchasing athletic equipment is a business proposition, and it should be conducted on a businesslike basis. There are certain procedures which are recognized as sound in any business. Although each school presents separate problems, there are certain fundamental principles of buying which will operate successfully in most situations.

Purchasing Equipment

The coach should always be consulted in the purchasing of athletic equipment for his squad. He knows the specifications, he understands what materials are needed and how they are to use, and he sees them tried and tested. He comes into contact with the problems which are presented by the equipment.

This practical experience with athletic goods enable the coach to make valuable suggestions and recommendations. The athletic director also plays an important role in the purchase of equipment. He may have far more experience with equipment than the coach, and if this is the situation, he should tactfully guide the coach in his recommendations. He must also determine that the equipment request is in line with the budget and that the amount and type of equipment ordered can be justified. In high school the principal usually has the responsibility of approving purchases of athletic equipment.

The superintendent also does this frequently, particularly in the smaller schools. The athletic council, board of education, and business manager of the school may also have this responsibility. In colleges and universities the approval of the athletic director is usually all that is necessary. However, the athletic council or the business manager may also give approval.

The inventory. Before athletic equipment is purchased the need for it should be carefully considered.

This will necessitate an itemized inventory of the equipment room covering both the amount and the condition of the materials on hand. Some directors can be rightly criticized for being unable to justify amounts of equipment purchased. The inventory is the best insurance against overbuying on some items and underbuying on others. The director and coach should always have first hand information concerning the amount and condition of the stock on hand, and an accurate idea of team personnel and requirements for the coming season.

Standardization of Equipment

"Standardization of equipment" is a common expression among directors. By this term is meant the adoption, by a school, of a certain colour, type, and style of equipment, which is maintained over a period of years. There are advantages in buying certain consistent types of equipment, usually from the same firm. It allows for replacement of the equipment in whole or in part. It maintains quality of material and colour. The end result is uniformity over a period of years. Economy is practised in that items can be matched in varied quantities without having to purchase a complete new outfit each season. Parts and replacements are easily obtained and repairs can be made more successfully.

The uniformity of equipment for team members adds colour to the organization and strengthens the team moral. There is no question that lack of uniformity may be interpreted as bad buying. The director must be alert to the rapid changes in equipment, however, in order that he will not be found with a large store of obsolete or extinct types on hand.

Quality Merchandise

It is consensus of informed opinion that, as a policy, the purchasing of the better grades of equipment is best. The most expensive equipment is not always the best, but it must be recognized that good material will be more expensive than cheap material. It has been proved on numerous occasions that quality merchandise fits better, looks better, wears longer, and can be repaired more advantageously than cheap items. The director must not go to the extreme in paying prices to the point that teams go unequipped on a limited budget, but experience has shown that in the majority of cases, low-cost materials are low-grade materials. The practice of purchasing cheap merchandise for reserve and freshmen teams has not proved to be economical. It is far better to pass down from the varsity squad quality material in good repair than to provide a cheap grade of equipment that may last for the season but gives little promise of being suitable for reconditioning.

Early Buying

The director should not overlook the advantages of early buying. Fall equipment should be ordered in the spring and spring equipment in the fall. Many colleges and high schools have their own peculiar designs in different articles of equipment and the manufacturer needs time to make these up. When ordered early, good workmanship is assured, but if the order goes in late, mistakes are more likely to occur. Another advantage of early buying is that the buyer has the opportunity to return goods that do not meet specifications. Materials that are not up to standard can be returned more conveniently when have been delivered early. Early buying also aids the manufacturer.

He is better able to estimate the expected volume of business and prepare for it. He can produce better materials at a better price if the labour is spread out over the entire year instead of being accumulated during certain intervals. In addition, the reputable manufacturer has the opportunity to replace materials that are defective or not up to standard.

By Within Range of Ability to Pay

This is sound policy in any business. Credit is easily obtained, and many directors have gone heavily into debt as a result of unrestrained purchasing. Even though many school operate on a budget, it is possible to spend more for equipment than can be afforded. Buying too much and too expensive equipment has plunged many athletic departments into debt. Buying too much equipment is not so serious a mistake as buying too expensive equipment, because the surplus can be used later. Many coaches and director have been overanxious to equip their teams with the best and have gone to the extreme in their buying. Although quality merchandise is advocated, small high schools cannot afford to by the same grade of equipment that large universities use. When a director over purchases equipment, the operations of the entire department may be curtailed, and his ability as an administrator is questioned. Frequently, schools by recklessly after financially successful years. As a long-term policy, consistent, regular buying is to be preferred.

Take Advantage of Legitimate Discounts

Many discounts which are offered to prospective buyers are, in reality, no discount at all. The amount of the discount is added to the original selling price in order that it might be taken off to attract purchasers. "Two per cent within ten days" is, however, a legitimate discount. The seller can afford to offer this discount for the advantage of being paid within ten days after the goods are billed. Practically all firms offer this discount and the director can save his department considerable money by taking advantage of it. Many of the larger institutions buy in the spring, but on a September 30th dating. The discount period carries up until October 10th, by which time football gate receipts are available to pay the bill and still take advantage of the discount.

Legitimate discounts may be secured if large quantities of athletic equipment are purchased at one time. The director should take advantage of this discount if his purchases are large enough to obtain it. Frequently, the larger universities ask various reliable companies to submit bids for supplying the athletic equipment. Considerable savings may result by this method of buying, as manufacturers are killing to reduce their selling prices for a larger volume of business.

Purchase from reputable concerns. There are bargains in athletic equipment as well as in other lines of merchandise. The director who knows athletic materials can recognize and take advantage of bargains when he encounters them. However, to be constantly hunting for bargains is a poor policy. Much time and effort will be wasted, and the bargains will frequently prove to be disappointments. Cut prices should be viewed suspiciously. High-grade merchandise cannot be sold consistently at a cut rate. Reputable equipment concerns sell to schools and colleges at reasonable rates and they cannot afford to make a practice of cutting prices. Reliable companies guarantee the excellence of their products and this guarantee is worth paying for. Few directors are accurate judges of textiles, leathers, and other materials used in the manufacture of athletic equipment. Cheaper grades of cloth, fibre, padding and leather can be made to look like better grade materials. Unless the director knows equipment thoroughly, he must relay upon the integrity of the companies with which he deals. Every director will discover that buying from reputable firms will prove more satisfactory and more economical as a long-term policy.

This does not mean that all goods should be bought from the same firm year after year. There are tendencies to form too strong an attachment for a particular manufacturer against which one must be alert. The quality and price of his goods may change to advantage or disadvantage. New materials and new processes may enable one firm to excel temporarily in certain items. It is better keep an open mind regarding the products of different manufacturers.

Official Equipment

Practice all games or sports have certain items of equipment that must be manufactured to specifications and are commonly marked "official." The specifications may call for a definite weight, length, relative dimensions, certain types of material, or the exclusion of certain materials. The purchaser should be acquainted with such specifications or any changes that may occur from year to year or season to season. Cases have occurred where competitors have been ruled out of an athletic event or records have been refused on the grounds that the implements used were not "official." This may have come about through the ignorance of the purchaser or the misrepresentation of a salesman.

How to Buy

The best buyers study market conditions for proper values. Equipment prices fluctuate and the director who knows when to buy and when to refrain from buying can save his department money. Although prices are fairly uniform among sporting goods houses, excellent values are frequently offered on certain items by the various companies. If the director and files the prices of equipment of the different firms, he can compare them when he is ready to buy. It is a fact that the most expensive materials are not always the best.

The most effective way to discover how equipment stands up is to use it and check the results. Some universities use spring football and freshmen teams as proving grounds for football equipment. If equipment rooms are properly managed, they should serve as laboratories to check the results of purchasing decisions. It is a simple matter to tag equipment and check it from time to time to see how it wears. The form on the following page is used at the University of Iowa for this purpose. Not only does such a check on the equipment show how it wears but it also indicates the amount of shrinkage of the items tested.

Local Dealers

Many directors are confronted with a situation in which they are expected to buy from local dealers or distributors. This becomes a problem when the local dealers cannot compete with the quality, price, and service of outside firms. When this is the situation the director should buy from the outside manufacturer, for he is obligated to deal where he can secure the greatest value per dollar.

It is a poor policy to make local enemies but it is a poorer policy to sacrifice school funds for personal protection. If the director can clearly demonstrate the advantage of purchasing from outside companies, it is a mistake not to do so. When local firms offer equal values they should be given the preference. In some schools purchases are made from local dealers if their prices do not exceed those of outside merchants by more than 5 to 10 per cent.

Purchasing in a Small School

The greatest need for wise buying is the small schools. Peculiarly enough, most of the poor purchasing occurs in the institutions which can least afford it. Service is the major factor to be considered in the small schools because the equipment must be used year after year. Very seldom are complete outfits bought for an entire first team or squad; a few uniforms or parts of uniforms are bought.

The best solution to the problem is to standardize the equipment and then purchase an excellent grade of material. Fancy, high-priced merchandise is impracticable for the small institutions. The small high schools cannot expect to equip their teams with the same grades of materials that the universities use, but the manufacturers have supplied strong, serviceable a equipment which is well suited to their needs.

Approval of Equipment by the National Federation

The National Federation of State High School Athletic Associations has taken a step to make more difficult the sale of unreliable equipment by dishonest companies. A joint committee of the National Federation and a number of leading sporting goods concerns have worked out a plan to establish certain standards of safety and to label approved equipment. Each of the firms agreed to make up a line of merchandise which meets the standards set up by the joint committee. Under the supervision of the standards set up by the joint committee. Under the supervision of the committee the materials and types of construction are tested in a United States government testing laboratory, and only those articles which satisfy rigid tests are approved. The approval is indicated by a federation tag and label, which are a guarantee that the materials are exactly as they are represented. The National Federation approval is withdrawn from any article which is found to be inferior. In case dishonesty on the part of the manufacturer is indicated, approval will be withdrawn from all products of that manufacturer.

Ordering Equipment

In any type of school, large of small, order blanks should be used in purchasing equipment. To order verbally is a poor policy. If the director or purchasing agent orders goods verbally he will probably fail to make a record of the transaction. When the merchandise arrives it cannot be checked accurately, and in case of a dispute the buyer will not be able to show just what goods were ordered.

If the director makes a practice of ordering goods by letter he should keep a carbon copy of his letter. Order blanks are preferable, however. They are uniform in size and can be filed systematically. Furthermore, it is desirable to use an order number which will check with the invoice number. The director who uses order blanks and keeps them filled will have a complete record of his purchases from which he can easily make reports for the season or year.

The samples on the following pages are suggested as guides in printing order blanks and vouchers. The usual letter size, 8½ by 11 inches, is commonly used.

The original copy of the purchase order is sent to the firm with two voucher forms, and the duplicate purchase order, which should be printed on coloured stock, is filed until the goods are received. With the duplicate blanks on file, the purchasing agent or director may readily check up at any time to ascertain when the goods were ordered. When the bill is paid the duplicate purchase order may be filed with the receipted voucher. When possible, goods should be ordered by catalogue numbers.

Most schools use voucher forms which have proved satisfactory. The original or white form is filed with the copy of the purchasing order to show payment, and the duplicate is returned to the shipper with the check to show that the bill has been paid. Some firms will return their own voucher forms along with the voucher which was attached to purchasing order. The vouchers provide for a statement of terms. When orders are placed a number of months or weeks in advance, it is well to state that goods are to be billed at a certain date.

At the lower left-hand corner of the sample voucher the word "Appropriation" is marked. This space should be used for indicating the sport or department to which the goods should be charged. The line marked "Rec'd O.K." is to be used when the goods are received by one person and the voucher is approved by another. At times, there will be mistakes in shipping, and when this is the case the fact will be noted in this space after the goods are unpacked.

There is a difference of opinion regarding the value of purchase order blanks and voucher forms in the smaller institutions. The volume of business in the larger schools necessitates purchase order blanks and voucher, but there is a need for system and businesslike procedure even when purchasing on a small scale. The cost of printing the forms is really insignificant when distributed over a period of years.

Purchasing Specific of Equipment

In this section we shall discuss some specific items of equipment and those features of each which the purchasing agent should bear in mind when making his selection.

Football shoes—The shoes are very important items of equipment. It is a sound principle to purchase the best shoes that the budget will permit, because, in the long run, it will prove economical. Inasmuch as there are so many different types of leather, tonnages, and construction features involved in the manufacture of shoes, it is particularly important to rely upon shoes from reputable manufacturers.

The Goodyear welt construction has been proven by long experience to be excellent for all-around serviceability. Because it is built around a leather insole this type of construction assures a good foundation for the shoe. This will enable it to take the wear and tear, mud, water, and perspiration without losing its shape. Moreover, it is always repairable. Kangaroo leather—either yellow or blue-black—is the preferred material for shoes uppers because of its light weight, great strength, moisture resistance, pliability, and durability.

However, this is the most expensive leather. Calfskin also makes and excellent leather for the uppers. Horsehide is a less expensive material for uppers. It does not possess the advantages of kangaroo or calfskin, but it is serviceable and stands up well.

Cowhide makes the best sole leather for football shoes because it is tough, water resistant, and does not readily scoffer crack. Fibre substitutes for leather should be avoided. Good leather that has been saturated with water will not become mushy or lose its original shape. Shoes with detachable rubber cleats have almost entirely replaced shoes with attached leather cleats. The cleats which screw into the sole are preferable to those which screw into a fixture mounted on the sole.

Helmets— Because of the serious nature of injuries to the head the football helmet is the most important piece of protective equipment. The protection afforded rather than cost, weight, or appearance should be the guide in purchasing this piece of equipment. As soon as helmets do not offer complete protection to the head they should be discarded. Such helmets should never be used for practice or handed down to reserve or freshmen teams.

Helmets are made of hard, outer shell, usually leather or plastic, which is capable of absorbing the hardest blows without dentine. The sell be well padded on the inside, preferably with sponge rubber. A web suspension in the crown has become popular because it distributes the shock throughout the helmet. "Helmets which have a canvas, leather, or rubber padding, regardless of their thickness, attached directly to the fibre padding, regardless of their thickness, attached directly to the fibre or plastic shell, furnish less protection to severe jarring than those with an air space between the foundation and the shell."

Football Pants—Football pants are made of a variety of materials. Canvas of eight-ounce weight per square yard has been a very popular material for this piece of equipment. It is a not so expensive as other materials. Whipcord and gabardine cloth are good materials football pants. If whipcord is heavily enough, it will not pick up water as readily as canvas; it will last longer, take colour better, and keep its bright appearance and sheen. The purchase of satin, silk, or balloon-cloth pants is not recommended if service is desired. They make a flashy appearance, but mud and lime, when allowed to dry in them, take out the colour and weaken the fabric.

Nylon cloth is being used increasingly for football pants. This material wears exceedingly well, holds its sheen indefinitely, cleans easily, is resistant to moisture, retains shape well, and, at the same time, weighs less than most other materials. Nylon pants are expensive, but in the long run they are economical.

As a policy, the purchase of shell pants will prove more economical if good materials are used. This type of pants is wasteful in that it will wear out much more quickly than the pads. It is advisable to buy shells and get good pads for them. The pads will outlast many pairs of pants.

The knees are the weak spots on almost all pants. It pays dividends to buy them with large leather knee pads. The leather should extend almost from seam to seam and come down close to the bottom elastic. The use of an elastic two-way stretch in the back of the pants reduces the strain on the knees and at the same time improves the fit. The coach also should be reinforced because it is subject to hard wear. Eyelit stays are also important. Stays should be faced with leather because laces will wear out the best cloth eyelit holes, and when this happens the pants keep sliding off the hips.

Basketball Pants—Basketball pants usually made from tackle twill, satin, and cotton, Nylon is not used extensively for this item of equipment. When it is used, the basketball pants should be lined because of the translucency of the material.

Jerseys—Nylon fabric has become very popular for football jerseys. It is usually combined with wool or Durene for this item of equipment. When it is used with wool, the great strength of nylon is combined with the absorption and warmth qualities of wool. It fits well, is elastic, durable, and holds colours well. The Durene-nylon combination provides a lightweight but very strong jersey. It cleans easily, is elastic, and holds its colour exceptionally well. Woollen jerseys are warm in cool climates and hold their shape well. They fit well and can be made up attractively in a variety of colour combinations.

It is a delicate fabric to clean. It is not durable. Like nylon, woollen jerseys are expensive. Knitting mills weave woollen in various grades and mixtures with other fibres in order to combine the best qualities of each. Cotton football jerseys are used by some schools during the warm weather early in the fall. In the south most of the schools wear the lighter jerseys, usually made up of the high-grade cotton or Durence, which is dressed-up cotton. As cotton is much cheaper than nylon or wool, some schools use cotton is much cheaper than nylon or wool, some schools use cotton jerseys for practice, if handed down woollen or nylon jerseys are not available.

Cotton jerseys are considered best for track. Rayon is extensively used for track and basketball jerseys. It is usually combined with cotton. It is an inexpensive jersey, holds colours well, is of medium weight, and is easy clean. Rayon is not a good material for football jerseys because it lacks durability.

White football jerseys are not advisable because they are difficult to keep clean. In addition, they are not so strong as other fabrics since bleaching weakens the fibres. White may be satisfactory for basketball and track but not for football. The raglan jersey, which is designed to fit over shoulder pads without stretching and strain, is favoured by many coaches. In purchasing jerseys of all kinds and T-shirts, it is very important to obtain neck sizes which are large enough. When the neck sizes are too small the jerseys and T-shirts are easily torn as the players pull them over their heads.

Shoulder Pads—Shoulder pads have been greatly improved in recent years. Kapok and foam rubber have replaced felt and rubber as padding. They both are excellent from the standpoint of protection. The foam-rubber pad is considered the best, but it is also the most expensive. It is not so durable as the kapok padding because perspiration causes it to lose its resiliency.

For this reason, if foam rubber is used it should be adequately treated for moisture resistance. Kapok is easier to recondition. The fibre part of shoulder pads should be water proofed. Fibre is composed largely of wood pulp and is susceptible to water, just as piece of stiff cardboard is. Unless the fibre is water proofed, it will break down if exposed to moisture and will no longer provide protection.

Both types of shoulder pads—the flat and the cantilever—have their advocates. Manufacturers claim that either type will afford equal protection. The fit of the pad is an important consideration. When the pad is placed on the shoulders it should fit snugly. The pads should fit down well over the chest and there should be a strap from the chest to the back protector to keep the pad snug.

Hip or Kidney Pads—Hip pads must be carefully purchased if they are to fit properly, provide adequate protection, and still not hinder various movements. They must protect the coccyx, the head of the femur, and the anterior-superior spine of the ilium. They are padded like shoulder pads with kapok and foam rubber.

Inflated Balls—Rubber balls of all types have been greatly improved in recent years, and since they are appreciably cheaper than leather balls, they have supplanted the latter in many instances. Rubber balls are used extensively in service classes and intramural athletics. Some interscholastic and intercollegiate teams employ them at times for practices. Rubber balls are durable, will not lose their shape, and will not pick up moisture. Because of this resistance to moisture, rubber balls are especially valuable for football or soccer practices which are held in the rain or on a wet field. Rubber basketballs, volleyballs, and softballs are also available.

Almost all leather inflated balls are made of cowhide, which does not stretch as much as horsehide. The difference in prices of footballs, basketballs, volleyballs, and soccer balls is due largely to the grade of leather that is used. The choice section of any hide is called the bend, which comes from the middle of the upper back of the animal. The section immediately surrounding the bend is termed back and is considered the second best part of the hide. The fibres in these two sections of the hide are more closely knit, stronger, and more firm than other types of leather. The third best leather is rump, and grouped together as the poorest types are shank, flank, and neck, these sections have fibres of varying lengths and are usually spongy and coarse. The best balls, with close, small, tight, and firm fibres, will keep their shape, but cheaper balls, or inferior leather, will not. One good ball will give greater service than two inferior balls.

Rackets—Rackets are made of a variety of materials. The preferred material for both tennis and badminton frames is well-seasoned, second-growth ash. Both types of frames are laminated. Steel tennis and badminton rackets are available, but apart from their durability, and thus reduced expense, they have no other advantage. Aluminium and fibreglass frames have just been made available, but further experience is needed before they can be properly evaluated. Plastic badminton rackets have also recently appeared, and these seem to be very promising. Rackets are strung chiefly with gut and nylon. Gut is preferred, but its cost limits it to the most expensive rackets. Nylon has almost entirely supplanted silk for badminton and tennis strings. It stands up well, is not affected by moisture, and is relatively inexpensive. Tennis rackets are strung with 15 and 16 gauge strings; badminton with 19 to 20 gauge strings. By stringing badminton rackets with 16 to 18 gauge strings considerable saving is effected because these heavier strings rarely break.

Shuttlecocks—Plastic shuttlecocks have been sufficiently developed so that they are satisfactory for all but expert players. They are much less expensive than shuttlecocks made with goose feathers. The development of plastic shuttlecocks has been a boon to badminton. Many schools have been able to introduce badminton into the service and intramural programs because of the greatly reduced cost of the shuttlecocks.

The Care of Equipment

A good equipment room is the first essential in the proper care of athletic equipment. A carelessly kept supply room can take a greater tool on the life of athletic equipment than many hours of hard service on the playing fields because athletic equipment spends most of its life in the equipment room.

The equipment room must be conveniently located adjacent to the locker and training rooms. It should be large enough to store all of the equipment of the department adequately and provide sufficient space for the handling and repairing of it. Proper lighting and heating are important. The equipment room ought to be well ventilated, dry, free from sweaty walls and pipes, and protected against moths, roaches, rats, and other rodents. The equipment room should be so constructed that shelves and bins can be built against the walls in order to have articles readily accessible for issue. Fairly deep shelves which will accommodate cartons and bulky articles are necessary. Narrower shelves for shoes and smaller articles are desirable. Enough shelves should be available so that nothing need be dumped in the corners or on damp floors. Steel bins and shelves are recommended.

A cage-door, sliding type of window with a counter is necessary. Every athletic department needs a drying room in conjunction with the equipment room. In almost all gymnasiums there is a corner in which an inexpensive drying room can be built. Placing wet uniforms in a locker after practice or a game will tend to rot the material and to rust the lockers. With the use of a drying room this problem will be solved, and the department will save a considerable amount of equipment. In addition, the drying room is a necessity if the department hopes to launder its own equipment and towels. A room 3 feet deep, 10 feet wide, and 8 feet high, lined with thin gauge galvanized iron, can be equipped at a small cost. Galvanized iron pipe is the most satisfactory material for hangers. It is wise to construct a protective shelf of galvanized pipe and wire about 3 feet above the floor to prevent articles from falling on the heating unit.

A 7-foot heater, equipped with six equally spaced 600 watt, 200 volt, screw-type electric elements, will supply adequate heat. Excellent ventilation map be assured by cutting eight 3-inch holes in the doors, 4 inches from the floor, and constructing the top of the room in a cone shape, with a small power fan installed in a 6-inch pipe that discharges the air currents out of doors.

The fan should run only when the heat is turned on. A drying room of this size will accommodate training shirts, shoulder harness, sweaters, pants, and socks for thirty-six football players or the entire uniform exclusive of training pants, for fifty basketball players.

Equipment Room Management

An equipment room manager is indispensable to the director and coach whose presence is required on the practice field or in the training room when equipment is most wanted by students. The universities and large colleges employ a full-time equipment room manager. A few large high schools are able to afford a full-time manager, but smaller institutions cannot. A part-time custodian may be employed or the janitor may take charge of the equipment. In most high schools the coach must assume responsibility for the equipment room. A common practice, however, is to appoint students to manage the equipment room. In some institutions the students are paid, but in many the students receive a manager's award for their service. Student managers are rarely as capable and proficient as full-time managers, but if they are carefully selected and trained, they will discharge their responsibilities satisfactorily.

If the equipment room manager requires assistance, he may be assisted by the managers of the various sports or by the student assistants. No other students should be permitted in the equipment room. If the equipment manager is to be held responsible for all of the equipment, he and his assistants should handle it alone. When everyone has access to the equipment the manager faces a hopeless task in preventing loss and preserving order.

Issuing Equipment—Every piece of equipment issued should be accounted for. A very desirable method of keeping a record of equipment is through the card system. Each student signs a card on which is recorded the equipment issued to him. Every sport has a special card of a different colour. On each card are listed the equipment is through the card system. Each student signs a card on which is recorded the equipment issued to him. Every sport has special card of a different colour. On each card are listed the equipment items which are issued for that sport. The football cards may be yellow and the basketball card white. After each card is signed it is filed alphabetically according to its colour. The chart on the following page is an example of a card which might be used.

At the beginning of the school year the equipment manager should assign all lockers, issue equipment to the students upon request of the director or coaches, and handle the daily routine task of managing the towel service. In the course of a season the equipment manager should inspect the playing equipment from time to time. This is done for the purpose of culling all equipment that is beginning to wear and of saving the athlete from possible injuries. The material that has been culled should be sent to the repair shop immediately.

This means of checking and repairing often saves the department considerable money. At the end of the playing season the equipment manager and his helpers check in all equipment. This can be done far better by clearing the lockers than by having each player check in his own equipment to the stockroom. There are always some players with more equipment than is charged against them, and this is the best method of securing it. Each piece of equipment, when checked in, should be tagged with its size and with the former player's name.

This saves the manager time the following season in giving it out to the returning players. Each article should be closely inspected, and those needing cleaning and repairing should be cared for at once. An inventory can be taken at this time in order to determine the equipment consumed during the season. A check can be made at the close of the season to see how the equipment has stood up in comparison with other makes during the previous years. Some schools check each player's equipment into the equipment room daily. Every player is given a number which is the key to the control of this system. This number appears upon the locker to which the player is assigned.

It is marked upon each piece of his equipment except the towel, quarter shirt, supporter, and socks, which are called white equipment. The number is also marked on the equipment except the towel, quarter shirt, supporter, and socks, which are called white equipment. The number is also marked on the equipment rack above each player's hook in the equipment room where his equipment is kept at all times. Only the white equipment is retained in the lockers. On reporting for practice, the player comes to the window of the stock room and gives his number to the equipment manager, who goes to the rack and brings the player all the equipment placed under that number. At the close of practice every evening the player returns his practice equipment to the window and the manager replace it upon the rack. The senior manager checks the equipment displayed under each number daily and, if any is missing, he endeavours to locate it. If any of the equipment is in need of repair, it is attended to immediately. The night before a game the practice equipment is removed from the racks and temporarily stored. Game equipment is substituted in its place upon the racks, and the player follows the same routine on the day of the game as he does for the practice sessions.

This is an excellent system of handling athletic equipment, and it is recommended if a large equipment room is available. All equipment which leaves the equipment room must be accounted for in some way. Coaches or their managers and instructors should sign for the equipment they use.

Students who check out balls and other equipment for free play should sign for it. Ordinarily, they are requested to return the equipment within a certain time and never to keep it overnight. The practice of students signing for equipment and then permitting other students to turn it in later should be combated. This frequently results in lost equipment. In some school each student checking out an article for free play exchanges it for one of his streak shoes which is not returned to him until the borrowed items are returned. All equipment should be numbered and each student should then sign for a numbered item.

Use of Equipment—The development of the proper attitude among all students regarding their athletic equipment is the most important consideration in the care of equipment. Much equipment is lost or damaged by carelessness or destructiveness. Frequently, varsity athletes do not feel an obligation to treat equipment carefully. Unless all students have a respect for property and are indoctrinated with a desire to care for their equipment properly, considerable unnecessary damage and loss will be incurred. Students must appreciate the fact that athletic equipment is loaned and not given to them and that they are responsible it is lost. Petty thievery can best be combated by making each player accountable for everything checked out to him.

Marking Equipment—All athletic equipment of an institution should be marked in some way in order to identify it. The usual way of doing this is to stencil or stamp the name or initials of the school on the equipment. In addition, athletic clothing should have the size clearly indicated on them. The identification of the school on athletic clothing does not suffice; the items issued to each player should be numbered and the numbers recorded in the equipment room. This is additional bookkeeping, but it helps to trace missing articles.

When this system is known to all the students within a school, it reduces the amount of stealing. Clothe articles may be successfully marked with a stencil and stencil point or an India ink stamp. Leather goods can be stamped. In some institutions initials are burned into leather goods, but unless this is done carefully, the leather will be damaged. Wooden items of equipment can be marked by burning initials at some convenient spot. Identification labels can be sewed into some articles. Many items of equipment may be purchased already marked. An additional charge is usually made for this service. It has been found, however, that it is more economical to purchase sweat socks with some mark of identification than to have it done within the equipment room.

Care of Specific Types of Equipment

It stands to reason that not all athletic equipment can be treated, cleaned, or stored in the same way. The materials from which the equipment is made—leather, rubber, fabric, wood, and so forth—require different methods of care. If the persons using it are to get the maximum service from the equipment he orders, the athletic director and his assistants must be familiar with the manner of caring for the various types of apparatus on hand.

Leather Balls—The Vulnerable part of any leather ball is the stitching. The stitching can be protected by relieving the pressure inside the ball between seasons. Slowly drying the ball when it is wet rather than forced drying will also protect the stitching. When inflating a ball with a rubber core valve, always moisten the needle, preferably with glycerin. If the needle is moistened with the mouth, remove the moisture from the needle after using it. A rusty needle will injure the core of the valve. The needle should be inserted with a gentle, rotary motion. A pressure gauge should always be used to insure correct inflation. Over inflation should be avoided, inasmuch as it strains the fabric lining and thus affects the shape and life of the ball.

A ball which has been used in the mud should be wiped clean with a damp cloth and then dried at the normal room temperature. Leather balls should never be placed near a radiator or hot-air register. To clean a ball which has been discoloured commercial cleaners or saddle soap are recommended. When the leather of a ball has become harsh and rough because of repeated exposure to moisture, and application of a commercial leather dressing or a light mineral oil will prove helpful.

Leather balls should be partially deflated when stored away between seasons. They should be stored in a cool, dry place without objects of appreciable weight upon them.

Rubber Balls—The Chief enemies of rubber are direct sunlight, heat, grease, and oil. With regard to sunlight and heat, all that can be done is to avoid exposure when possible. Grease and oil should be removed with soap and warm water. Dry-cleaning fluids should never be used on rubber goods. Rubber balls should be stored in a cool, dry bin or box away from heat or sunlight.

Textile fabrics. Bourquardez and Heilman have made a thorough study of the care of textile fabric. Their recommendations. All woollen items must be protected against moths. Moths will not attack nylon or cotton fabrics. After jerseys are cleaned, they should be stored away by sizes. The should not be stored in open bins where dust will collect but in closed containers with moth repellent.

Leather Goods—The most common sources of trouble with leather goods are high temperature and excessive moisture. There are three types of formations which accumulate on leather, only one of which is harmful. This is green mold which rots leather. In order to prevent green mold rot, leather articles should be kept in a cool, dry place. When wet, leather equipment should be dried immediately, but the action should not be forced. The article should be dried at normal room temperature without the use of artificial heat. Sun drying and air streams or pressure should never be used. The proper care of leather shoes is especially important.

They are subject to dampness due to perspiration, rain, or snow. This condition tends to remove the training oil from the leather, causing it to dry out and crack. In addition, shoes if worn when very wet become misshapen. In caring for wet shoes, lime and mud should first be removed. Warm water should be used if necessary. Oil or grease should then be applied and worked into the leather. Castor oil is especially recommended.

If the oil is warmed before application, it is more efficacious. Oil should be applied to the uppers, and wool grease to the soles. It is important to keep oil and grease away from rubber cleats. Wearing football, baseball, and track shoes on stone or concrete floors should be discouraged.

Before leather shoes are stored away after the season they should be cleaned and oiled. The should be oiled again about the middle of the year. The toes should be stuffed with paper to help the shoes retain its shape. The shoes should be stored in special compartments to promote air circulation and to avoid crushing.

Wooden Equipment—Wooden equipment such as bats, golf clubs, hockey sticks bows, and lacrosse sticks, are built to last for long periods of time and will do so when properly handled. Moisture is the main source of difficulty. It will damage the wood where the finish has worn away. Consequently applications of warm linseed oil are recommended whenever the finish of the wood requires it. Javelins and vaulting poles should be stored in such a manner as to prevent warping. Storage of wooden equipment in a cool, dry place is recommended.

Nets and Rackets—Nets which are exposes to dampness will rot. Nets which are used outdoors should be tarred. If they are dipped in creosote every year, their life will be prolonged. The should be taken in during bad weather, kept dry, and repaired at the first indication of damage. If space is available, it is better to hang tarred nets on pegs in a cool, dry area rather than fold or roll them. Badminton and tennis rackets should always be kept in presses when not in use. Restraining is much less expensive when it is done immediately after a string has been broken. Probably the greatest source of racket problems is too great string tension. This condition greatly increases string breakage and loss of shape of frames. At the same time it does not improve the performance of the poor and average players. Expert players use tightly strung rackets, but such equipment is neither necessary nor desirable in physical education and intramural activities. A tension of from 50 to 60 pounds is adequate for such use.

Badminton Shuttlecocks—Badminton shuttlecocks should be kept in a moist environment. The feathers lose their oils in a dry atmosphere. A humidifier is recommended for the storage of a considerable number of shuttlecocks. The greatest damage to shuttlecocks comes through careless use. Students Should not be permitted to abuse this fragile equipment. Shuttlecocks are also saved when students are prevented from smashing and swinging vigorously until they have developed proper skill and timing.

Archery Tackle—All bows should be unstrung when not in use. On the archery range the bow should be hung on the ground quiver between rounds. When not in use, the arrows should be racked in a dry place. The rack should be so constructed that there are three pressure points on the arrow—one two inches from either end, and one in the middle—to prevent warping.

Helmets—Helmets should be cleaned before they are stored away. Dirt and hair oil should be removed by using saddle soap or a commercial ball cleaner. In storing helmets the important consideration is to maintain their shape. Throughout the year they should be carefully stored on special racks, or they may be stuffed with newspaper with head trees on the inside and suspended from wires close to the ceiling. The should not be hung by the chin strap. Helmets should not be crushed by having heavy objects placed upon them or by having individuals sit upon them. Throwing helmets is also a practice which should be prevented. The common practice of carrying helmets in a duffle bag is not recommended.

Hip and Shoulder Pads—These items of equipment should be cleaned and repaired before being stored. Hip and shoulder pads can be washed with warm water and soap if care is used to avoid getting too much water into materials, such as kapok, which absorb it. Leather parts should be lightly oiled after cleaning. Special forms are easily made upon which shoulder pads may be stacked. Stacking pads more than five or six high will spread the arches of the bottom pads to the point where they lose their body-conforming shape. If space is available, open wooden racks to accommodate not more than two pads to each space is the ideal arrangement. Hip pads should be hung by the belt loop.

Mats—The two common practices which are harmful to gym mats are rolling or bending them in any way and dragging them on the floor. Mats should always be kept flat. When they need to be moved they should be carried by the handles or transported on a mat truck.

Canvas mats should be cleaned once a month with a vacuum cleaner. If they are heavily used and become grimy, they should be cleaned with a commercial mat cleaner. Tears in the body or the handles and broken tufts should be rapaired immediately. When the mat cover is beyond repair, it is less expensive to have it recovered than to purchase a new mat.

Track Equipment—Metal shots should be cleaned with steel wool and oiled before being stored away. Steel tapes should be treated similarly. Discuses should be cleaned and shellacked, than placed in a rack, and stored in a room that is not overheated. Javelins should always be hung from a height with the point downward to prevent warping.

School Laundry

The great amount of laundry service which physical education departments need every year, particularly for towels, runs into large sums of money. More and more schools are finding they can reduce this expense considerably by installing laundry units and doing their own laundry.

Cleaning Uniforms

The great majority of institutions must relay upon commercial cleaners to launder their athletic uniforms. This is a specialized type of work which requires trained personnel and proper facilities. The athletic director would be well advised to seek a cleaner who specializes in this type of cleaning.

Athletic uniforms are among the most difficult to clean garments known to the cleaning industry. They are subjected to dirt, perspiration, rough usage, and a variety of stains—grass, blood, resin, iodine, and adhesive tape. In addition, practically all items of the uniform consist of two or more fabrics, each of which may require separate handling.

Sporting goods manufacturers recommend that the athletic director take a complete uniform to the cleaner in advance of the season to prepare him for the type of cleaning it will require. If the cleaner knows the fabrics involved in the various parts of the uniform, whether or not rubber is used, and the colour fastness of the garments, he is much more likely to clean it properly.

Repairing Equipment. Athletic directors would profit by investigating thoroughly the possibilities of repairing their own equipment. The extent to which it is should be repaired depends upon the size of the school and amount of athletic equipment handled. In some of the larger institutions the stockrooms are so completely equipped that all athletic equipment can be repaired. The practice in the majority of schools is to make simple repairs and to send the remainder to local repair companies or national reconditioning concerns. Many schools could cut their equipment bill appreciably by enlarging their repairing facilities.

A sewing machine that can sew leather as well as textile materials is indispensable in the equipment room. Such a sewing machine will more than pay for itself in a short time by mending the rips and tears which occur so frequently in all types of athletic materials. Special facilities for sewing football, basketballs, and baseballs by hand should be available also. Another excellent way to repair rips and tears in cloth or canvas in by Lam-A-Fab, a newly invented liquid fabric cement. Anything made of fabric is quickly, cheaply, and permanently repaired by this product.

It is particularly useful in repairing gymnasium mats. The repair of shoes is important. The shoes should be inspected frequently in order that damage may be detected at its beginning. Detachable cleats should be shifted around so that they will wear evenly and be of uniform height on all shoes. When the cleats are shifted, the fixtures should be checked to ascertain that they are tight. The old cleats should be used on the practice shoes and the new ones placed on the game shoes.

It frequently occurs that when one shoe is useless

for further wear, its mate is still in fair condition. These odd shoes should be saved for replacements. Common sense must be used repairing equipment. Up to a certain point it is good economy to recondition athletic materials, but beyond that it is a waste of money. Some directors make the mistake of repairing old equipment that will not give them enough service to pay for the repairs made. It is more advisable at times to sell old equipment to cleaning and reconditioning firms and apply the money to new equipment. In the great majority of schools only minor repairs can be made on athletic equipment.

The practice has developed of sending all equipment in need of repair to special equipment reconditioning companies. A number of these have developed in all sections of the country. Originally, many of these firms were not adequately prepared to do effective work, but most of those which have survived have developed the personnel, the specialized equipment, and the technical skill to do a superior job of reconditioning athletic equipment.

8

Significance of Efficient Office Management

Every physical education administrator needs to understand the essentials of efficient office management. This need is obvious in large department, where secretaries, clerks, telephone operators, and receptionists are available to provide a variety of service for the public and the department personnel. However, the same functions must be carried on the a one-man department, where no secretary or office equipment is available. Regardless of the size of the department, correspondence must be carried on, reports rendered, materials duplicated, equipment ordered, materials filed, and records maintained. Whether the department is large or small, the internal requirements are the same.

The only difference is that in the small department the administrator must do more things himself, and in the large department the various duties are delegated to others to perform. There are proper and improper ways of performing all the office details in physical education office. To do them correctly saves both time and money. The efficient operation of a department requires sound office procedures. Such procedures have been tested and proved in business and industry and may be readily adapted to school situations. No administrator can afford to fail to use them.

Office Functions and Practices

The size of the physical education office usually varies with the size of the institution and the extensiveness of the program. In some very small secondary schools the physical education administrator is fortunate to have an office. In many other small school, if he has an office, it is one which he shares with several other staff members. Office personnel, if any is available, usually consists of a part-time secretary or volunteer student secretary or clerk. At the other extreme are the physical education administrators in large colleges and universities who have several secretaries, a telephone operator, and perhaps even a receptionist—all housed in commodious offices with the latest types of equipment.

Regardless of the size of the office staff and facilities, there are many functions which are common to practically all offices. These are:

1. Filing.
2. Keeping appointments and meeting obligations.
3. Answering and placing telephone calls.
4. Duplicating materials.
5. Receiving visitors.
6. Answering correspondence.

Each of these functions will be discussed briefly.

Answering and placing telephone calls. In larger offices telephone calls will be placed and answered by the secretary or telephone operator. The administrator without office assistance must perform this function himself. In either case standard telephone technique and courtesy should be observed. Favourable or unfavourable impressions of the department are readily created by the manner in which telephone calls are received.

The proper procedures do not accidentally occur—they must be taught and insisted upon by the administrator. The individual answering the telephone must be as friendly and as cordial as if the caller were a visitor in the office. Courtesy and helpfulness are essential. Good public relations are created when the receiver of the call demonstrates a willingness to do whatever is required. Since emotions are readily reflected in one's voice, care must be exercised not to show anger.

When it is necessary to give a negative answer the caller must have the feeling that the has been courteously treated. The telephone should be answered promptly. The department should be identified immediately. The name of the person receiving the call is frequently given. For example, "Department of Physical Education, Miss Smith speaking." Such terms as "Hello" and "Yes" are not used in answering telephone calls in a business office. A pencil and telephone pad should be available to take massages or telephone numbers which are to be called. If the administrator is not available, the secretary may be able to provide the desired information herself. If the administrator is occupied, the secretary should have an understanding with him regarding interruptions.

When the administrator leaves the office, he should let the secretary know where he can be located and when he expects to return. When he is out of his office, a form similar to the one given above should be used to indicate that a call has been received in his absence. If the person called is not in, the secretary should always offer to take a message. It is helpful to get the name of the caller if he does not identify himself. In such instances the questions "May I have him call you?" or "Mr.———is not in. Is there a message?" are in order.

Office Unit Orientation

The administrative offices should be centrally located so as to be accessible to all who have business with the director or any of the staff members. Almost invariably the office is located near the entrance of the gymnasium or the physical education building. Staff offices should be located adjacent to the central office and close to the classrooms. The desirability of having a large central office serving as a work room for the secretarial and clerical staff, as a repository for all departmental records, and as a reception room for visitors is evident. In addition, a conference room should be available for staff and committee meeting, conferences, and as a place for the entertainment of guests. However, neither of these facilities will be found in most high schools.

Receiving Visitors

Every members of the clerical staff should be well versed in the common courtesies of greeting visitors as they call at the office. Needless to say, all visitors should be made welcome. They should be cordially greeted, and every effort should be made to meet their needs. In the event the caller has no appointment, the purpose of his visit should be determined. If it is necessary to wait to see the administrator, the caller should be comfortable seated. Something to read should be offered him. If the administrator is not available, either an appointment should be arranged or an effort made to have someone else provide the assistance the visitor desires. Visitors with appointments or important visitors should be announced immediately. A courteous procedure should be worked out whereby the secretary interrupts an unnecessarily long interview with a visitor, especially when other visitors are waiting. She can enter the office and announce, "Mr. Smith is here for his ten o' clock appointment. When there are no callers, an effective procedure is to summarize what has been discussed and to inquire there are other matters to be considered.

Answering Correspondence

One of the quickies ways for an administrator to gain a poor reputation is to be negligent or careless about answering his correspondence. Some administrators have a policy of answering every letter within twenty-four hours after it has been received. Although this may not be possible in all cases, it is a sound practice to answer correspondence promptly. Not only should the answer be prompt but is should be complete as well.

All questions should be answered carefully and in good English. Needless to say, all letters should be answered. Many letters which the administrator receives can better be answered by some other members of the department. A from is usually employed, requesting the appropriate action by the staff members. Many letters of a routine nature can be answered directly by the secretary.

This well save the valuable time of the administrator. In larger institutions letters of the same type are commonly received. These may be answered by a standard form replay. It is standard procedure to proofread all outgoing letters to detect mistakes. The address should be checked for accuracy. Carbon copies are necessary, and they should be filed with the related correspondence. When the letter contains enclosures, its weight should be determined to insure proper postage. Each letter should be examined to determine whether it has been signed. Unless the letter is neatly and correctly executed it should not be forwarded. No administrator can afford the unfavourable impression which a smudged, carelessly written letter will produce. In many small school the administrator will have no secretarial help whatsoever.

In these situations he must handle his own correspondence. If he is unable to type, his only recourse is to write out his letters longhand. The other extreme occurs where a full-time or part-time secretary is available to take shorthand. In between these extremes are the schools in which dictaphones are available. Dictaphones have several advantages. They can be taken home and letters dictated at nigh or over the week end. Administrators who have part-time secretaries can dictate at any time and have the completed cylinders available for the secretary when she arrives.

When the administrator is constantly interrupted during dictation, or if he has difficulty composing a letter, he can save the time of his secretary by using the dictaphone. If the administrator has a student or an inexperienced secretary, he must remember to dictate slowly. In addition, he should have the secretary read back to him the material that has dictated. He should also check the letters carefully before he signs it.

The administrator should save the time of his secretary by having everything in readiness for dictation. If any reference data are necessary, they should be obtained prior to summoning the secretary. It is poor economy to have a secretary unoccupied because she is waiting to take dictation.

Filing

An effective filing system is essential in any office. All of the correspondence, records, budgets, and reports must be filed in such a way that they can be located quickly. It is not difficult to locate recently filed material, but on occasions several years may elapse before it is needed. Reference to filed material is constantly necessary, and when it cannot be located, delay, inefficiency and, at times, embarrassment result. Filing is more accurately done when only one person does it. A variety of filing systems are known, but in school the alphabetical system is almost invariably used.

The material to be filed is classified according to name, subject, or a combination of name and subject. Large physical education office will probably use both a name and a subject file, but the great majority will use the combination system. The name file refers to names of people or organizations with whom correspondence or business is carried on. Individuals are filed under their surnames. The alphabetizing is continued through as many letters as are necessary to differentiate the names. Prefixes such as De, Di, Mac, Mc, Von, and O are part of the name they precede. In this system a folder is made for each name or correspondent if there is sufficient material to justify starting a folder. From three to ten papers justify starting a folder.

A lesser amount is filed in a miscellaneous folder. A miscellaneous folder is made for each letter of the alphabet and is located behind the last name folder under the particular letter. Any material for which there is no separate name folder is filed in the miscellaneous folder, alphabetically rather than by date. Subject filing refers to filing the material according to the subject matter with which it deals. The subject headings must be specific, significant, and technically correct. Nouns are generally used to refer to the subject. Subheadings are used in subject filing. A miscellaneous folder is also used in subject filing.

The papers in a subject folder are arranged by date, with the latest date on top. When subject files are used, the maintenance of a separate alphabetical list or card index of the subjects is recommended. This will prevent filing material under a new heading when a folder is already available. A subject file is necessary in any physical education office because of the nature of its operation.

Items such as budgets, schedules, contracts, equipment orders, records, and reports must be filed according to subject. Since there are many more items which would be filed under subjects than under names, most physical education offices should file by subject into which names are incorporated. This may be done by including correspondence in the miscellaneous folder in a special correspondence folder. However, if extensive correspondence is carried on, a separate name file should be maintained. In any filing system cross references are necessary to locate various documents.

This is useful when reference is made to a specific document that might be filed under several headings, and a cross-reference form should be placed in the folder under the related designation. The cross-reference form should be mimeographed on 8½ × 11½ inch paper that is coloured. It should allow for (1) the correspondent's name, and (2) data to indicate to what letter or document reference is made. When a file is removed from the filing cabinet for any length of time an "out" slip or guide should be inserted. Regular "out" guides have pockets for the cards which indicate the location of the missing file. When individual papers are removed from the files, an "out" slip should be substituted. An "out" slip should be wider than regular paper so as to clearly show above the edges of the other papers within the folder.

When folders or papers are not returned promptly to the files but are kept at various desks, it soon disrupts the filing system. Secretaries must keep their filing up to date. When they are busy, there is a tendency for a considerable amount of unfilled material to accumulate on their desks. In setting up a filing system for a medium-sized school, the first step should be to segregate the total program into specific subjects, such as:

1. Physical education.
2. Intramural sports.
3. Health education.
4. Interscholastic sports.

Each drawer of a four-drawer filing cabinet would refer to a specific area with the subareas listed in alphabetical order. The physical education drawer could be subdivided into the following areas:

1. Committees. A folder for each committee should be filed.

2. Departmental policies. The departmental policy file should be included in a folder. If desirable, a number of folders might be used with each including the policies in different areas.

3. Annual reports. A folder for each annual report should be included.

4. Budget. A folder for each annual budget for each of the past five years should be maintained.

5. Correspondence. Folders should be arranged alphabetically under this heading. All carbons and original copies of communications should be filed in the appropriate folder.

6. Financial matters. Duplicate copies of all requisitions and duplicate vouchers submitted for payment can be filed under this heading.

7. Equipment. A folder should be included listing the equipment, excepting that included in the interscholastic inventory. The new equipment on order should also be noted.

8. Student help. Records for all part-time and student help should be kept in this folder.

9. Personal records. A folder for each student should be available. This should include his medical examination records, correspondence with family physician, parents, and others. Excuses and the anecdotal record of student achievement and conduct can also be filed in this folder.

10 Test data. Complete data on Physical fitness and other tests should be filed in folders according to the school year in which they apply.

11. Service program. A folder for each activity taught should be available. This might include lesson plans, rules, syllabus, examinations, and teaching aids, such as clippings from newspapers and magazines. In addition, a folder for the program and schedule for each year for the past three years should be included.

The Intramural Sports Drawer could be Subdivided as follows:

1. Publicity. A folder should be retained which has all the posters, announcements, news stories, and other publicity materials.

2. Programs. A folder should be available which would contain the details of each year's program for a period of five years. The details should cover such items as the participants and teams in each sport and the results of all the competition.

3. Schedules. This folder should contain schedules for all intramural activities for the current year.

4. Intramural activities. A folder for each sport included in the program should be available. These should included rules governing that activity. In addition, it might include past records and schedules.

5. Officials. A folder with the names, addresses, telephone numbers, and qualifications of all officials used in the program should be available.

The Health Education Drawer might be Arranged as follows:

1. Health instruction. A separate folder under this subject heading should be available for each of the following areas: personal health, communicable and non-communicable disease, first aid and safety, family life education, nutrition, exercise, rest and recreation, health service and products, community health, and narcotics and alcohol education.

2. Administrative policies. A folder under this heading should be included for each of the following areas: communicable disease control, emergency care and injuries, excuses, health of school personnel, and scheduling.

3. Healthful school living. A separate folder under this subject heading should be included for each of the following areas: school lunch, seating, heating, lighting, ventilation, swimming pool sanitation, and locker and shower room sanitation.

5. Health services. A folder under this subject heading should be included for each of the following areas: health examinations and follow-up, screening, counselling, communicable disease control, and sanitation of the school plant.

The interscholastic sports drawer might be subdivided as follows:

1. Contracts. A folder is desirable for each sports which involves contracts.

2. Budget. A folder should be filed for the interscholastic athletic budget for each year for the past five years.

3. Transportation. Folder should be developed for each sport. Every folder should contain all arrangements

for travel by the respective team.

4. Sports. A folder for each interscholastic sport should be maintained. Included in such a folder will be squad personnel, current records, lesson plans, scouting reports, coaching aids, and the like.

5. Schedules. Schedules for all sports in the current year should be included in the folder. Folders for previous years should also be maintained. In some schools a folder for future schedules in needed.

6. Officials. All data relating to officials should be filed under this heading in folders arranged according to sports.

7. Game reports. A folder for each sport should be included which would contain game reports for home games. The game reports should include such data as attendance, weather, gate receipts, opponent, and score.

8. Equipment. A folder for each sport should be available in which data concerning equipment is filed. These data should include an equipment inventory plus a listing of new equipment which has been ordered.

9. Eligibility lists. For each sport, a folder should be available in which there is an eligibility list.

From time to time the files should be checked and obsolete material removed. It does not take long for the files to become cluttered with useless documents unless they are cleared at periodic intervals, say annually or semiannually. Some of the material can be discarded completely; other papers may be transferred to an inactive file. How long various documents are retained depends somewhat upon the nature of the material and the space available in the filing cabinets.

Duplicating materials. A constant need exists in a physician education office to have materials duplicated. In addition to the requirements in instructional classes for objective examinations, reading lists, syllabi, instructional materials, and outlines, coaches may wish to have plays duplicated for their players, and the intramural director will require numerous copies of rules and schedules. The administrator will also need to have various materials duplicated, such as departmental regulations, announcements, minutes of committee meetings, and instructions to staff members and students. In most high schools and colleges the materials are mimeographed or dotted in a central office.

However, when the volume justifies it, the physical education department has found it advantageous to possess its own duplicating equipment. Dittoing equipment, particularly, is inexpensive to purchase and to operate. Although the ditto and mimeographing machines are simple to operate, it is advisable to restrict their use to authorized individuals only. On staffs where little if any office personnel is available, staff members can learn how to operate the duplicating machine. They can then reproduce their own materials.

Keeping appointments and meeting obligations. On many occasions physical education administrators must make appointments to speak to people or to perform some task by a certain stipulated time. To meet these obligations the administrator must have some infallible system of reminding him of these events. He must use the techniques which have proven successful in all types of offices. He simply cannot afford to miss or to be late for an appointment, forget details, or submit trade reports. The establishment of regular office hours facilitates the making and keeping of appointments.

When staff members, students, tradespeople and others know what the regular office hours are, they can usually arrange to see the administrator at a mutually convenient time. He must keep his secretary informed concerning any changes in his office hours, especially when he knows he will be absent or late. When the necessity of performing a task occurs, many administrators endeavour to take care of it immediately.

If the administrator is free for an immediate appointment, or can make a telephone call, write a letter or prepare a report at once, rather than defer it, there is no possibility of forgetting it. If the matter cannot be immediately disposed of, a notation should be made concerning it. Calendars are essential in any office to assure that appointments are kept and obligations met. The administrator needs a desk calendar with 15 or 30 minute time designations. All appointments and obligations should be noted on the calendar.

Every office has a number of recurring items every year, and these should be noted on the calendar at eh beginning of the school year. The administrator also needs a pocket appointment book. This should include all the notations which are on his desk calendar. He will made appointments when he is away from his own office. He will also need to know of his office appointments when he is elsewhere. It is essential that the appointments on his desk calendar and pocket calendar coincide. If a secretary is available, she should also maintain a desk calendar.

It is her responsibility to see that her calendar and those of the administrator are accurate, identical, and up to date. She must be careful to learn of the appointments that the administrator makes when he is away from his office. She must see that the administrator meets all his appointments and obligations. To remind her employer of a task he should do, the secretary should place the file on his desk. If it is obvious that he has overlooked a call or appointment, she should remind him of it. It is a sound practice to spend the first few minutes each morning with the secretary, discussing the daily schedule. Some secretaries place a typed schedule of the administrator's appointments on his desk every morning. Whenever the administrator leaves the office, his secretary should be aware of where he might be reached and when he expects to return.

When he leaves his office at the end of the day, he should check his calendar to see whether he has any early appointments the following day. It is a mistake for the administrator to rely upon his memory for the conduct of his daily affairs. It has been said that "the shortest pencil is better than the longest memory." Everything that cannot be taken care of immediately should be written down is such a way that it will not be forgotten. A very helpful office device which may be combined with a desk calendar is known as the office tickler.

The tickler carries reminders for certain routine activities. There are in every department many duties which recur each year. These can be indicated on the office tickler in advance. The tickler file usually consists of a box built to hold 3 × 5 memorandum cards. A tabbed guide for each month and 31 tabbed guides for each day of each month are needed. Each activity which is to be performed at a future date is noted on the appropriate card. The cards are filed according to dates. The tickler file needs to be checked every morning. Certain items which occur frequently throughout the year can be handled by a single card.

Thus, if the payroll must be completed on the last day of each month, the same card may be used each month, rather than making twelve separate entries. Another task which can be handled by the secretary is making travel arrangements. The secretary needs to know the approximate time of departure and return, the mode of travel, accommodations desired, appointments, and hotel preference. With this information, she is able to make all arrangements and save considerable time for the administrator.

In larger office secretaries make the necessary arrangements for committee meeting. To work out a convenient time and place for a number of people to meet is frequently a time-consuming process.

Office Management in a Small High School

The heavy load of the administrator in a small school makes good organization and efficient methods of office management particularly necessary. He should have one period set aside every day for the conduct of his departmental affairs. If such time is not provided, he will need to use his free period or time before or after school.

Whatever assistance the administrator has will come from students. Fortunately, in most high schools it is possible to obtain senior students interested in office work who will volunteer their services to gain experience. It is not difficult to find students who can type and some are capable of taking shorthand. The administrator will probably need to use several students to accomplish all the necessary probably need to use several students to accomplish all the necessary duties. In this way the duties which require special skill can be reserved for the period when the student with that skill is available.

It is relatively easy to teach the student clerks how to use the telephone, to receive visitors, to file materials, to use mimeography or ditto machines, to maintain records, and to perform the essential housekeeping duties of the office. They can render invaluable service if they are used wisely. They must be given recognition for their services, and care must be exercised not to exploit them.

In the small high school office equipment is usually limited. The minimum items in any office should consist of:

1. Extra chairs for guests.
2. Magazine stand.
3. Bookshelves.
4. Several card files of different sizes.
5. A four-or five-drawer filing cabinet with lock.
6. A large work table for student assistants
7. Calendar and memorandum pad.
8. One desk for each teacher.
9. Desk tools.

Office Management in a Medium-sized High School.

In a medium-sized high school the physical education administrator has the same duties as the administrator in the small school. However, he is much more likely to be allocated time for his administrative duties. He may be relieved of two or three teaching periods per day for this purpose. More office equipment will probably be available. He will undoubtedly have more people to whom he can delegate various duties. It might be possible to use the principals' clerical staff for dictation, typing, and mimeographing. Student assistants will continue to be needed. For part-time and student secretarial help, a specific job description will be helpful. If they can have recourse to written instructions and policies concerning their various responsibilities, they will avoid many mistakes. A typewriter and typewriter table and a telephone and an alphabetical index to common telephone numbers should be available in the administrator's office.

Office Management in a Large Institution

In a large school where one or more clerical personnel are available the role of the administrator is that of office manager. All the activities carried on in the office are his responsibility. The duties of the different individuals are assigned and supervised by him.

A standard procedure in large offices in to develop a job description for each member of the clerical staff. This enables the employee to know specifically what is expected of him and that he or she to know specifically what is expected of him and that he or she is held responsible for demonstrating competence as it applies to these responsible for demonstrating competence as it applies to these responsibilities. This does not mean that each employee is restricted from assuming other duties in the office as circumstances require.

In a large office a definite organizational structure

might be necessary for the office personnel. Responsibility must be vested in some individual—usually the most experienced, mature, and highest-ranking member. The administrator will not have the time to concern himself with the details of managing the office. The assignment of duties, distribution of work, and supervision of the work of all office personnel should be delegated to this person.

The administrator is responsible for the development and maintenance of high morale and esprit de corps among the office personnel. He accomplishes this by creating pleasant work conditions, be establishing reasonable standards of accomplishment, by providing suitable working tools, and by friendly, helpful supervision.

In large schools the matter of communication practice is to use written inter staff memoranda. Special forms are available for this purpose. These memoranda are time saving and have the advantage of fixing responsibility. In addition, they reduce the risk of misunderstanding and error.

The Secretary

An important asset which many administrators overlook in planning their work is a capable secretary. By working with an intelligent secretary and learning to delegate to her all the responsibility which she is capable of assuming and by leaving in her hands many time-consuming routine matters, the administrator will find that he has much more time for creative work and will thereby be of much greater value to his profession. The wise administrator, then, should know what a good secretary is, what she can do, and how to make the best use of her abilities.

It may seem a bit obvious to state that intelligence, personality, and character are the three general personal qualifications of a good secretary, but the lack of any one of these dooms many an otherwise promising girl to the rank of the automation who "takes dictation." Her intelligence should be practical and analytical, not merely abstract, and she should be able to comprehend the factors in any situation and make some reasonable decision about it, with sound logic to back up her judgment.

Her intelligence must include a capacity for detail and an ability to deal with the almost endless routine matters which arise in any administrator's office. And if this intelligence is to function to the best advantage for the secretary and the administrator, back of it must be a real interest and pride in the activities, welfare, and progress of the department. If she is desultory and detached regarding her duties and performs them mechanically, she will be no particular asset. When an administrator has a secretary who is dedicated to her position and takes a deep personal interest in the success of the department, he is indeed fortunate. The personality of the secretary is of critical importance. She constantly encounters students, staff members, other faculty, and visitors, and it is vital that she create a favourable impression. Since the administrator will spend from on third to three fourths of his working hours in her company, it is axiomatic that her personality be an important consideration to him.

The pleasant, cheerful, and sensible girl is not only easier to work with than the temperamental on but will usually accomplish much more in the same amount of time. The caller's first impression of the administrator comes from the front office, where he is received by the secretary.

She is the office hostess and, as such, should have all the prerequisites of any hostess graciousness, cordiality, interest, and tact. By her own well-bred manner and well-groomed appearance, she should convey the impression of the well-run office where all demands are given courteous attention. She should meet people easily and pleasantly and attend to their wants as effectively as possible, making no obvious display of efficiency, but quietly accomplishing what needs to be done. She will need endless poise, good humour, and diplomacy in dealing with the many who come to the office, and she must also exercise discrimination in determining which of them have legitimate business with her employer and which of them do not.

In a word she must be efficient, but charmingly so. Her telephone voice and manner should be as pleasant as her office personality. She should be able to convey to the person who calls that he is taking to a capable and willing person who, in most cases, can supply him with the information he needs without troubling the administrator about it. To assume the somewhat belligerent "who wants to talk to him?" attitude is as rude as it is inexcusable. The secretary who really becomes a part of the organization must be extremely adaptable and ready and willing to do whatever must be done, no matter how far it may seem to fallout of her sphere of activity.

She must remember that her position exists because she can be of service to the administrator, and that service is never limited to the mere mechanics of letter waiting. If She is to rise above the ranks of the typists, she will find herself sorely needing a sense of humour to enable her to keep proper perspective on herself, her job, and those around her. She must be able to talk easily and entertainingly on occasion, but above all, she must learn to be a good listener and to take an active interest in the discussions of the plans of the present and future which her employer will want to talk about to someone who understands what it is all about but who can be trusted to keep his confidence.

To be worthy of the name, the secretary must be absolutely reliable in all situations so that her employer may trust her as completely as he does himself. Her loyalty to him must be absolutely unquestionable. In the course of her day's work a secretary learns many things which are not for publication, but no matter how prone she may be to gossip about her friends and neighbours, she will never under any circumstances gossip about office information, however trivial it may be.

The necessity for personal integrity is too obvious to need statement. The training of the good secretary should be more than a matter of shorthand, typing, filing, and office practice, although these, of course, are essential. Most important is a knowledge of the English language and its correct use, which must include spelling and diction. Since she will compose numerous letters which will go out over the signature of her employer, she should have an appreciation of style and form in composition in order to make her letters convincing. She should know the essentials of order and have a systematic way of getting her work done, not only in the quickest way but in the best possible way.

She should sense the relative importance of each task and learn to do first things first. It is desirable but not essential that she have some training in the field in which her employer is interested. If this is not feasible, she should acquire at an early date a very real interest in that field and keep herself reasonably well informed about it.

This will not only add to her enjoyment of her work will increase her value to her employer. Having hired a secretary, many an administrator seems to feel that his responsibility is ended, and from on it is up her.

If he takes that attitude, he will soon find that he does not have a capable secretary but just one more girl working in the office. It is important that as soon as she begins working, he should see to it that she has all possible information concerning the work that is to be done.

In any organization there is almost endless red tape with which the secretary becomes entangled in the course of her day's work, the workings of much of which she will eventually learn by trial and error. But a knowledge of the regulations will save her endless time and trouble. Do not expect her immediately to assume charge of all the routine matters which will arise. Give her time to learn. But gradually, as she proves herself capable, delegate to her all the responsibility she is able to handle.

Much has been written of loyalty of the secretary to her employer, but much more might be written about the loyalty of the employer to the secretary. She is, presumably, intelligent and capable of handling her job, and she should be backed up by her employer in any reasonable situation, not made the scapegoat for all the mistakes which occur in the office. To humiliate her in order to inflate one's ego before important callers is, of course, and inexcusable but not uncommon practice.

9

Relationship of Health Education and Physical Education

Many people regard health education and physical education as synonymous or one as being part of the other. This is an entirely erroneous impression. Health education and Physical education are separate and distinct, though closely allied, fields. Physical education is that phase of education which comes about through or in connection with vigorous muscular activities. Health education, on the order hand, comprises all of the experiences which contribute in any way to the individual's health knowledge, health habits, and health attitudes. Health education differs from physical education in subject matter, methods, and in some purposes. Physical education has important contributions to make to health education, and vice versa.

Inherent in physical education are exceptional

opportunities to develop health knowledge, health habits, and health attitudes. On the other hand, the emphasis in health education on such areas as exercise, nutrition, recreation, rest, and desirable health practices has important implications for physical education. However, a lecture in health education or a trip to the local dairy is not physical education, nor is a unit in basketball or wrestling health education.

Changing Outlook on Health

Schools have broadened the scope of their program considerably in the last half century. Modern philosophy considers that an educational institution is concerned with more than the intellectual development and vocational preparation of youth. Experience has clearly shown the inadequacy of an education which has been limited to only these objectives. Health has come to be considered one of the most important of the objectives of education.

Health is too important to be used to individual or family initiative. Education realized that whatever other objectives are sought, health aids in progress toward them. Health is basic to learning, to happiness, to success, to effective citizenship, and to worthwhile living. Without health, the individual is less effective than he might have been and is handicapped in everything he does. Some persons with poor health have made significant contributions to society, but these contributions have come in spite of their handicaps.

World War II greatly increased the importance of the health objective. The lack of health and physical fitness of American men and women was one of the major revelations of the war. The selective service medical examinations revealed all too clearly that insufficient attention has been given to health. Although some progress hand been made, the nation was shocked that we had profited so little from out experience in the previous war. Public opinion was aroused, and all health agencies accelerated and expanded their activities. The schools have responded to the challenge and are emphasizing health to a degree never before approached.

Modern concept of Health. When educators first made a place in he curriculum for health, they regarded it only as physical soundness. An individual was ill when confined to his bed—otherwise, he was well. The emphasis was on freedom from disease and physical defects. As time passed, more and more was read into the meaning of health. It was found that a psychosis or neurosis was more detrimental to the health of an individual than flat feet and that emotional breakdowns were as serious as physical breakdowns. This broadened concept of health is expressed in the definition:

Health is considered that condition, mental and physical, in which the individual is functionally well adjusted internally as concerns all body parts and externally as concerns his environment. The definition of health is positive; it means more than merely keeping out of the hospital. It implies a healthy organism and a healthy personality.

The Objectives of the School Health Program

The aim of the school health program is the development of optimum physical, mental, emotional, and social health among all pupils. The specific objectives which lead to the accomplishment of this are outlined by Anderson:

1. Development of an appreciation of aesthetic factors related to health.

2. Acquisition of scientific and functional knowledge of personal and community health.

3. Development of healthful personal practices.

4. Development of wholesome health attitudes.

5. In each youngster a positive health awareness and a desire for a high level of health.

6. Reduction in the incidence of communicable and non-communicable diseases.

7. Special health provisions for the exceptional child.

8. Detection and correction of all defects and disorders.

9. Prevention of defects and disorders.

10. Development of the highest possible level of health for each youngster.

11. Supervision and guidance of the health of the children.

12. A continuing appraisal of each child's health status.

13. An understanding of each child's health needs.

14. Provision of emergency measures.

15. Establishment and maintenance of sanitary practices and surroundings.

16. Mentally hygienic school environment.

17. Effective social adjustment.

18. Development of a high level of self-esteem in each

youngster.

Organization of the School Health Program. Since health is so educational in function, it is very important that its supervision and control be centred in the board of trustees or board of education. In the past, many communities placed the responsibility for the public health work in the board of health. The board of health has the machinery for the control of communicable disease and can administer this phase of the program better than the board of education. Considering the educational aspects of the school health education program, the control should reside in the board of education, but there should be co-operation with all local groups interested and concerned with health. The best way of bringing about school community co-ordination and co-operation in matters relating to the health of the school population is through a community health council.

This council should be composed of representatives of the schools, the local board of health, the county medical and dental association, and all other public and private agencies concerned with health. The community health council concerns itself with broad policies and problems and mobilizes all the health resources of the community behind the school health program. A health council or health committee should be organized, where possible, in each school.

The function of the health council is to give guidance and leadership to the health education program within the school and to co-operate with the community health council through duly appointed representatives. Membership on the health council co-ordinator, various teachers, and student and parent representatives. If a school psychologist, nurse, nutritionist, and dentist are available, they should also be included. Every school must have a physician who will function as a school medical adviser.

Small schools will be unable to afford a full-time medical adviser, but it will be possible for them to obtain one on a part-time basis. It is essential that every school have resource to a physician to advise upon the many health problems which require medical judgment. In many communities where the school is unable to afford a paid medical adviser, the county medical society will frequently co-operate by contributing the part-time services of several physicians without charge. There must be someone within each school who has a definite responsibility for the total school health program.

This individual is known as the health counsellor or health co-ordinator. Every school should have a health counsellor or health co-ordinator. In the smaller school and colleges the co-ordinator may be any instructor, head of department, or, in the case of high schools, the principal or superintendent. Regardless of the size of the institution, the best qualified individual should be in charge of the health program. The director of physical education is frequently the health co-ordinator. Educators have associated physical education closely with health values and objectives. Unless the physical educator is well trained for health education there is no justification for placing him in charge of the health education program.

If he has been well prepared, however, he is in a strategic position to perform excellent service. Students usually esteem him highly and grant him great authority, particularly if he is the coach. He comes into close informal contact with the boys and thus gains a better understanding of their health problems and needs. The woman physical educator, too, can get closer to the girls than any other teacher. Innumerable opportunities occur in the physical education classes and intramural and interscholastic sports to protect, promote, and teach health.

In the smaller institutions the physical examination is usually conducted by the physical education department. For these reasons the physical educator makes an excellent health co-ordinator in the small schools if he or she is well trained. Teacher-training institutions are providing much more adequate preparation in health education than hitherto, and in the future physical educator will be better qualified as health co-ordinators. In the large institutions the task of administering the physical education department requires so much of the director's time and effort that it is inadvisable for him to undertake the additional responsibilities involved in directing the health education program.

The health co-ordinator. The success of the school health program depends to a great extent upon the health co-ordinator. He should have the following qualifications and training:

An understanding of the purpose and functions of all health agencies in the community, particularly the local public health organization.

Training in special skills required in health education, including the methods and material and information, the nature, preparation, and use of visual aids, public relations and publicity methods and techniques, and the nature of the printing and duplicating processes and their use.

1. An appreciation of the potential contribution of all subject-matter fields and all other phases of school life to the total health program.

2. An Development of the nature and functions of the total school health program.

3. Thorough preparation in the field of the health, including personal health, nutrition, mental hygiene, first aid, health and physical diagnosis, and communicable disease control.

4. A strong preparation in education, including educational psychology, principles of education, educational methods, curriculum construction, and tests and measurements.

5. A strong basic science background, including physics or chemistry, biology, physiology and bacteriology.

The duties of the school health co-ordinator usually involve the following activities:

1. To see that students needing special attention are refereed to the school physician.

2. To help secure the most effective utilization of the school physician's time.

3. To assume the responsibility of the follow-up of medical and dental examinations.

4. To ascertain that the school physician's recommendations for special program for certain students are implemented.

5. To interpret to teachers the results of physical, medical, dental, and psychological examinations of their students.

6. To co-ordinate the school health program with all pertinent agencies and individuals, including parents, public health agencies, family physicians, and the local medical society.

7. To assume the responsibility for developing and supervising the total school health program.

8. To set up procedures for the evaluation of the school health program.

9. To assume the responsibility for the school safety program.

10. To work out detailed procedures to be followed when accidents occur.

11. To give leadership to the health instruction program. This involves curriculum revision with all those who teach special health courses; preparation of syllabi; assistance in obtaining films, books, and health instruction materials; and provision of in-service training where necessary. It also means co-ordinating the efforts of all teachers whose courses offer excellent possibilities for correlating instruction.

12. To secure publicity for the school health program and to see that all staff members are aware of the services available to them.

13. To maintain all health records of students.

14. To analyse the health factors involved intruancy and excessive absence and to take appropriate action.

15. To assume the responsibility for checking the

sanitary environment of the school.

16. To check students who return to school after illness or injury and to assist in their readjustment.

17. To determine that students who participate in extracurricular activities can do so without adverse effects upon their health.

18. To assist teachers who have pupils or advisers with health problems.

19. To make arrangements early in the school year for screening tests for vision, hearing, and posture.

Personnel. Health cannot be effectively taught in two or three periods a week. The entire staff of the school must protect, promote, and teach health every day in every way if a genuine contribution to the health of the child is to be made. A health-conscious staff is essential to a successful program.

The health personnel may include physicians, dentists, dental hygienists, psychologists, psychiatrists, nurses, oculists, nutritionist, other specialists, and visiting teachers. There are no accepted standards as to the size to the staff, although physicians, dentists, and nurses are considered necessary. The size of the staff is dependent upon what the school board and the community want and are willing to pay for. It is desirable that all of the health staff have some educational training in order that they have an educational viewpoint.

Health Education Responsibilities of Physical Education

The majority of physical education is secondary school and colleges and universities have important responsibilities in regard to the school health education program. Each must co-operate fully with the school doctor, nurse, or other medical personnel. Many physical education teachers participate in the administration of the medical examinations. Studies have shown that more physical educators teach the separate health courses than do any other teachers. A survey by the Federal Security Agency revealed that in forty-two different states physical education and health education are taught by the same certified teacher.

All physical education teachers have the responsibility in their physical education classes for teaching health habits, health attitudes, and health knowledge whenever a favourable opportunity presents itself. Because of their excellent background, many physical educators serve as health counsellors, particularly in the smaller schools. Finally, physical education and health education are combined into one department in many schools, and the physical education director has the responsibility for administering both programs.

Because of these important and varied relationships to the health education program the physical educator must be familiar with this important area. This is particularly true for the administrator in physical education who bears the responsibility for implementing all of the health education obligations of the department.

The Scope of the School Health Program

The major phases of the total school health program are: (1) healthful school living, (2) health service and (3) health instruction. Although each of these major areas is discussed separately, it should be emphasized that all are so closely related as to form parts of one co-ordinated whole, and only by such co-ordination can a worthwhile program be developed.

HEALTHFUL SCHOOL LIVING

Healthful school living is a more inclusive term, to be preferred to those which formerly designated this phase of school health education. This term refers to the entire environment which surrounds the pupil. It not only involves safe and sanitary facilities but also includes careful planning of the school day for study, play, and rest. Since teachers are also part of the school environment, the establishment of healthful teacher-pupil relationship is an important aspect of healthful school living.

Wholesome School Environment—Every school is obligated to surround its students with a healthful environment: physical, social, and emotional. Intelligently planned, hygienically arranged, well equipped school plants kept in a sanitary and safe condition are essential in the development and protection of child health. Construction and maintenance of the school building should be in accordance with standards established by law and by official building and health regulations. Adequate and well-arranged lighting and seating, properly functioning heating and ventilating systems, reliable equipment for fire protection, approved plumbing, suitable acoustics, adequate toilet facilities, and sanitary drinking fountains are some commonly recognized requirements for a healthful school environment.

Furthermore, adequate hand washing facilities, hot and cold, water, liquid or powder soap, and paper towels are all necessary for pupils as well as for teachers. Standards for school sanitary facilities are established in building codes of state education departments and sanitary regulations of state health departments. These standards were determined by experts, and if they are up to date and adhered to within a school, the proper physical environment for children will be assured. The responsibility for sanitary inspections may be that of school nurse, school doctor, health officer, or sanitary inspector, principal or superintendent. In smaller schools, the health co-ordinator superintendent may make the inspections.

The Organization of a Healthful School Day. The health educator has more control over the organization of a healthful school day than he has over the environmental conditions of the children. Any organization of the school day must be considered unhygienic if it overtaxes school children mentally or physically. Some of the factors which must be regarded by the health counsellor are these:

1. The student load.

2. Extracurricular activities.

3. The number, length, and kind of rest and relaxation periods.

4. The amount and kind of homework and the importance attacked to it.

5. The placement of the activities.

6. The length of the school day.

7. The number and kind of study periods.

8. The number and the length of the periods.

More high school and college students have had their health affected adversely by poor organization of the school day and unsatisfactory teacher-pupil relationships than by unhygienic surroundings. High school and college students need guidance in regard to the scholastic load they are carrying. They are frequently prone to undertake a heavy extracurricular load as well as other outside work. Some supervision is necessary to prevent them from understating too much.

The extracurricular participation may be restricted, the scholastic schedule may be lightened, or, if possible, the outside work may be reduced if the student demonstrates that he is carrying too great a load. The daily schedules of high school and college students should be such as to establish a regular program of work and insure sufficient time for meals, sleep, rest, exercise, and recreation. The college scholastic work should be limited to approximately eight hours per day or forty hours per week. The scholastic load should be about six hours per day in the high schools. Six periods of from 55 to 6 minutes are preferable to eight 45-minute periods. When the long period is used, there should be a "mid-period stretch" for several minutes. Part of the 60 minute period is used for supervised study, which tends to reduce the amount of homework. Five or six hours of home study per week is all that can be expected of high school students. When the 45 minute period is used, two of the eight periods should be devoted to study or activity periods.

Teacher-pupil Relationship—Every teacher in the school has a contribution to make to the health of the pupil. In addition to instructing and supervising the health by his teaching methods. The methods of teaching are particularly important from the standpoint of mental hygiene. Too much stress should not be placed upon term examination as a basis for promotion or final grades. The policy followed in regard to rewards and punishments should be considered carefully. Unwise disciplinary measures may have serious mental hygiene implications. The instructor should use fear as a last resort only to motivate desirable attitudes and conduct. Insofar as possible he should so conduct his classes that of failure, ridicule, sarcasm, or embarrassment may not result. He must recognize that constant failure invariably causes poor mental hygiene. The instructor is confronted with many different personalities, and he cannot treat them all alike. Teachers who understand the principles of mental hygiene and put them into daily practice make an indispensable contribution to the health education program.

The Teacher's Health—The highest attainable health of the body, the mind, and the personality of every school child is the aim of the health education program. Such an aim could hardly be attained by unhealthy teachers. For years teachers were assumed to be healthy when, in reality, they were not. The school has as much right to demand physical fitness from its teachers as intellectual and moral fitness. Not only is it incompatible for a teacher in poor health to teach, but such an individual amy even prove a source of contagion to the students. An unhealthy instructor is a health liability to an educational institution. High school and colleges have been giving more and more attention to the matter of the health of the instructional staff. In the past, the school itself was responsible for many of the factors which impaired the teacher's physical fitness. The heavy teaching load, the unhygienic lighting and ventilation of the school room, inadequate salaries, lack of rest rooms and rest periods, and dogmatic, destructive criticism were factors unfavourable to health. Other causes of ill health include hurried eating, insufficient recreation, poor living conditions, and lack of exercise.

The teacher's health may be promoted and safeguarded in a number of ways. Following are some recommended procedures for maintaining and improving teacher health:

1. Health insurance.
2. Teacher tenure.
3. Periodic physical examination, including a tuberculin test and a chest X ray for positive reactors.
4. Retirement fund for teachers.
5. Provision for health instruction for teaching staff.
6. Desirable, healthful living quarters for teachers.
7. Medical and hospital care for teachers.
8. Sanitary and healthful teaching environment.
9. Insurance of salaries during illness.
10. Adequate salaries.
11. Recreational facilities for teachers.
12. Rest periods and rest rooms.
13. A reasonable teaching load.
14. Health qualifications for new teachers.

SCHOOL HEALTH SERVICES

Nature and Scope of Health Services

This service program embraces the various protective measures assumed by the school to conserve and improve the health of children. The highest attainable physical, mental, and emotional health of every school child is the goal of the school health services program. The health services vary considerably in different institutions, but the minimum essentials of a good program include the following activities:

Health appraisal:

(a) The periodic medical examination.

(b) The periodic dental examination.

(c) Psychological examinations.

(d) Screening tests.

(e) Teacher-nurse observations.

2. The follow-up program.

3. Communicable disease control.

4. Emergency care procedures.

5. Health supervision of school personnel.

6. Student excuses.

7. Additional health services.

The scope of the school health services is limited in the curative and remedial field because of the non-educational aspects of this type of activity.

Health Appraisal—The total assessment of the health status of the school child is called health appraisal. Health appraisal is defined as "the process of determining the total health status of a child through such means as health histories, teacher and nurse observations, screening tests, and medical, dental, and psychological examinations. Not only do the physician, dentist, and nurse play a part in the health appraisal but the parent, teacher, and psychologist are also involved. The term health appraisal is a broader and more comprehensive one than physical examination, health examination, or medical examination.

• The periodic medical examination. The medical examination is that phase of health appraisal which is performed by the physician. A periodic medical examination is the very foundation of the entire health program, as health protection, health instruction, and health promotion are all dependent upon it. By determining the health status of every student, the medical examination may be used as the basis on which to plan the student's curricular and extracurricular activities or as yardstick to measure improvement in health and to guard against impairment of health. Cases of communicable disease must be discovered in order that their transmission may be checked and treatment obtained. The ideal program is one in which the examination is done by the family physician and the results reported to the school.

The parents and pupils are thus taught that medical care and supervision are their responsibilities and not those of the community. In addition, the family physician is better acquainted with the pupil, and more time and opportunity are available for a through examination. Family physicians should employ the same examination record form which the schools system uses. The students who are not regularly subjected to an examination by their family physicians should receive one from the physician serving the school. If a school physician is not available there are usually some local agencies which can arrange to take care of the needy children.

A recommended standard is medical examination every three years. A minimum standard is one as a preliminary to entrance to the kindergarten or first grade and one at the beginning of the fourth, seventh, and tenth grades. Previously the recommended standard was an annual medical examination. Experience has shown that this standard was impractical. Those schools which were attempting to meet this standard were often providing such a superficial examination as to invalidate the procedure. Less frequent but more through examinations produce better results. Qualified physicians and nurses should give the examinations, although the faculty and reliable students may assist in some of the routine details, such as weighing and measuring.

The time of the physician should be devoted as much as possible to those aspects of the examination which cannot be done by anyone else. Women physicians should examine the girl students. A satisfactory examination requires from twenty to thirty minutes for each student. A minimum of fifteen to twenty minutes of the physician's time should be given to each individual. The child should be stripped to the waist or clothed in a slipover. Privacy is essential if the fullest confidence of the student is to be secured. Preliminary to the examination, all available health records of the student should be brought up to date and reviewed. Each pupil should have a cumulative health record throughout his school career. Excellent forms have been developed for this purpose.

In addition to the data from the periodic medical and

dental examinations, the cumulative record should include the family health history, the health history of the individual, his health habits and complaints, symptoms and signs of health disturbances which he reports, teachers and nurses observations of health, attendance record, and the results of all psychological tests. During the examination, the physician should attempt to secure the confidence and the co-operation of the student.

It is desirable, particularly in the elementary grades, to have the parents attend the medical examination. Every effort should be made to schedule the examination when parents can attend. They can help the examiner to obtain a better understanding of their child and his health habits. The parents will discover the health status of their child, and they can ask questions which have been troubling them. The educational aspects of the examination should be interpreted to the students and to the parents. The examiner will lose an invaluable opportunity if he fails to commend the student upon the favourable aspects of his health and his good health habits. The medical examination should be quite complete.

If a blood test or urine analysis is needed, it should be done privately. Both these tests are too expensive for most schools to provide routinely. Some provision should be made for detecting tuberculosis. Many schools administer the tuberculin test and X-ray the positive reactors. Schools can obtain specialized assistance from local, state, and national organization devoted to tuberculosis control. Participation in intercollegiate athletics should be contingent upon passing an adequate medical examination.

The recommended standard is an examination of the participants prior to be beginning of each sport. The minimum standard is an examination once each year with a re-examination for those who have suffered a disabling injury or illness. The general examination which is ordinarily given to students is not thorough enough for athletes.

The medical examination of athletes should include an examination of the heart, pulse, and blood pressure before and after exercise, the lungs, bones, joints, and the inguinal and umbilical region for hernia. A urinalysis is strongly recommended. A tuberculin test, followed by an X ray for the positive reactors, should be required.

The periodic dental examination—The periodic dental examination is another essential aspect of the health appraisal program. This should be started in the preschool period and should be continued after children start in school. Early dental care will enable the dentist to discover and correct conditions before they become serious. At the time when children's temporary teeth are being replaced by permanent teeth and when they are so susceptible to dental caries annual visits to the dentist are recommended. The School's responsibility in regard to dental health involves the encouragement of children and their parents to see their dentist at regular intervals.

It also includes, in many communities, the conduct of dental inspections. A dental inspection is not complete as a regular dental examination in the dentist's office, but it does serve the purpose of discovering dental conditions which require correction. Many schools routinely provide dental inspections, but others do not.

Dental hygienists often administer the dental inspections. The trend is definitely to place the responsibility for dental treatment upon the parents. Special arrangements are usually possible for the children of destitute families.

Psychological Examinations—Another important aspect of health appraisal is related to the mental and emotional health of the pupils. This is a significant aspect of health and one which must not be neglected. Tests of intelligence, reading, social adjustment, personality, and attitudes toward school and other children are very helpful in providing additional data which relate to the health of children. In addition, the classroom teacher is able to report anecdotes, particularly of those children who deviate from the normal. The school administrator, psychologist, counsellor, guidance teacher, social worker, health educator, physician, and nurse may have valuable date to add to the cumulative health record in regard to the mental and emotional aspects of health. The mental health program is concerned with the discovery and prevention of mental and emotional illness.

In the discovery of such conditions the classroom teacher plays a vital role. Her close association with students throughout the school year gives her an exceptional opportunity to understand them. If the teacher has a good preparation in child growth and development and understands child behaviour, she will be able to detect children who depart from the normal. A knowledge of the factors which lead to mental and emotional illness is important in the prevention program.

One of the most important considerations is that the

child experience some success in his school activities. Constant failure is damaging to anyone's mental and emotional health. Providing an opportunity for each pupil to be creative in ways natural to him is another important factor. Satisfying relationship with classmates is also indispensable for the well-adjusted child.

Screening Tests—Screening tests are so-called because they "screen out" pupils who may be in need of further examination. Such tests are utilized particularly for height, weight, vision, and hearing. The screening process is usually done by the classroom teacher or non-medical personnel and enables the physician to concentrate upon those who most need his services. The classroom teacher performs the weighing and measuring at stipulated intervals. She also gives the vision screening tests. She may also give the audiometer tests for hearing if she has had special training to do so. However, specially trained personnel usually give this test.

Teacher-Nurse Observations—Teacher-nurse observations are also an important part of health appraisal. The teacher particularly comes in constant contact with students, and she can quickly determine whether her students demonstrate any symptoms of disease. If each home-room teacher inspects her students during the first period in the morning the early symptoms of health disorders may be discovered. Frequently, the teachers are not qualified to perform these inspections, but they can be trained in service.

Instruction in these techniques can be given to the teachers by the school nurse, health co-ordinator, health official, or physician. Every member of the faculty should be acquainted with the symptoms of communicable disease, such as coughing, sneezing, unusual polar, flushed face, running nose, headache, sore throat, nausea, skin eruptions, and inflamed eyes.

In addition to these, there are other symptoms of health defects, such as squinting or expressive blinking of the eyes, discharging ears, granulated eyelids, earache, inattention, and the like, which the teacher must learn to recognize. If the teacher observes some signs of disease or health defect, she should take the case to the school physician, the school nurse, or the principal.

Every school should have some individual who can make a more thorough examination of the suspected cases and authorize them to be sent home or to remain in school. The teacher should never be expected to make the decision as to whether or not the pupil should be excluded from school. When the individual is sent home from school, the parents should be notified of the reason.

They should be urged to secure medical attention, and the nurse or visiting teacher should ascertain whether the service of a physician have been obtained. When the student is able to return to school, he should have a certificate to that effect from his doctor.

It is recommended that the students be examined also by the school physician or nurse before being readmitted to class. The control of communicable disease is made more difficult in schools where undue emphasis is placed upon perfect attendance. The real tribute belongs to the child who protects his classmates by staying home when he does not fell well.

The Follow-Up Program

The value of a medical examination depends in a

large measure on the follow-up program. In too many institutions the results of the examinations are recorded, filed, and forgotten. The number of defects which are corrected after the examination is far more important than the number of defects discovered by the examination. In regard to the correction of defects there are two principles which must be recognized:

1. Any corrective work must be made an educational procedure.

2. No school health service must take away the fundamental responsibility of the parent.

The school is an educational institution, and not a hospital or clinic. The school is not prepared for curative or remedial services and should minimize its activities in this field. The responsibility for the school staff school staff should render first aid in emergencies and then call for the services of the family physician if further attention is needed. The only corrective work to be undertaken by the school must be educational in nature.

Adapted or corrective physical education falls into this category. The department of physical education provides corrective classes in which those individuals with physical defects and organic disturbances which are amenable to correction by physical modalities are given certain exercises or activities to remedy their condition. Instruction and practice in various recreative activities in keeping with the individual's defect are also given. If the parents are unable to be present at the medical and dental examinations, they should be notified by letter of the findings, and suggestions should be made concerning future examinations, treatment, and care.

It is well to invite the parents to visit the school and confer with the school physician on the examination results. Instead of sending a letter, the school nurse may visit the come and report and interpret the results of the examination and the recommendations of the examiner. At school, the results should be interpreted to the students and their individual needs pointed out. The teachers should be informed of the health status of their pupils and the steps which should be taken to remedy the defects. Teacher nurse conferences should be regularly scheduled.

They are usually most valuable if devoted largely to review and exchange of information regarding specific cases of children who seem to be in serious need of medical care, follow-up, or special study. The fully informed teacher can be most helpful both in adjusting the classroom program to the student's needs and influencing his and his parents to obtain correction of the remediable conditions as recommended by his family or school physician. The correction of all remediable defects found on the medical and dental examinations is the chief purpose of the follow-up program.

When the family cannot or will not assume the responsibility for correcting the defects, the school should bring the fact to the attention of public health authorities and social agencies. All agencies contributing to child health should be co-ordinated and their services brought to the attention of those families who are unable to pay for the attention of the physician. The school nurse or the visiting teacher is usually in the best position to make the arrangements between the family and the welfare organization.

Communicable Disease Control

The local health officer is the legal representative of the state board of health which has full power in the control of communicable disease. He consults with the private physician when the illness affects the community or school. He informs the schools concerning the current rules, regulations, and policies for the control of communicable disease. He plans jointly with the school administrator for the immunization and testing program, in co-operation with the private physicians in the community. He advises school officials concerning the exclusion from school of pupils or teachers because of exposure to or presence of communicable disease. The superintendent or principal is responsible for giving the school staff adequate interpretation of the most recent public health practices and for developing for their guidance procedures that are based on these practices.

Written and printed instructions with reference to the teacher's role in communicable disease control should be placed in the hands of every teacher in the school. The school administrator collaborates with the private physicians and public health officials in formulating plans of the schools. He also keeps parents informed about the school's policies and procedures, usually by letter and group meetings. One of the most important considerations in communicable disease control is the immunization procedures which are employed.

It is a recognized fact that artificial immunization through vaccination is highly effective against smallpox, diphtheria, tetanus, whooping cough, and polio. Despite this fact, a large portion of the school population is unprotected against these diseases. If the immunization program operated as it should in the preschool years and in the elementary schools, the problem of immunization in high school and college would be reduced considerably. Parents should be encouraged by every means possible to have their children immunized their family physician in their preschool school years.

It is recommended that the smallpox vaccination be administered to children before their first birthday. The diphtheria, whooping cough, and tetanus immunization is recommended for children from three to six months of age. This can be done at one time by means of the triple antigen, which provides protection against all three diseases simultaneously. The practice of postponing these protective procedures until the children enter the elementary school should be strongly discouraged.

The public must be educated to the value of artificial immunization and the necessity of having it done early. The real facts should be placed before the public through the newspapers, school publications, letters, visits by the school nurse, and parent-teacher meetings. Religious objections and ignorance are the chief foes to be combated. The schools should co-operate with the public health program of promoting immunization. As each child enters the elementary school his needs in regard to immunization should be determined.

The necessary information is obtained from the family physician on a form which is sent to the parents. Some children will not have had any previous immunization. Those children which have been previously immunized will require booster injections. Whatever the needs of the children are follow-up procedures will be necessary to see that proper immunization is obtained. Parents are expected to assume this responsibility through their family physician.

When the family cannot afford this expense public health or social agencies are available to handle it. Some colleges and universities give vaccinations as part of the service for the student health fee. Others make no charge for it and vaccinate those needing it as part of the entrance examination. During epidemic the public health agencies or the school usually furnish emergency inoculations.

Emergency Care Procedures

All school should be prepared to render first-aid treatment in the emergency situations which occur so often. The school doctor should prepare detailed instructions and standing orders for the guidance of the teachers and nurse with reference to the procedure in handling common school emergencies.

If they are not available, first aid should be given by some member of the teaching staff who is qualified to do it. All teachers of physical education, shop, health, driver-training and safety education classes should be certified in Red Cross first-aid training. In the event of a serious accident, the school doctor or any other physician easily and quickly obtainable should be called immediately. The names, addresses, and telephone numbers of nearby physicians who may be called in emergencies should be posted in the principal's office. After first aid has been given, the parents should be tactfully notified of the child's accident.

The parent should indicate what hospital, physician, or home address the sick or injured child should be taken to if the parent himself cannot promptly call for the child. The sick or injured child should never be sent home unaccompanied by a responsible person. If the parents cannot be reached, the family physician should be called. There should be on file in the school the name of each pupil's family physician, whose notification in case of emergency has been authorized by the child's parent. The best qualified individual should be prepared to help an uncertain parent decide what is next to be done for the child. All school personnel should clearly understand that they should not go beyond first-aid treatment of an accident or illness. They should not diagnose or administer medication of any kind unless prescribed by a physician.

Health Supervision of the School Personnel

The importance of a healthy school personnel has already been pointed out. The school health service has the responsibility for supervising the health of the teachers, the custodians, the secretaries, and others who come into contact with the students. The medical examination should be given annually for the school officials as it is for the students. The follow-up program for the correction of defects should be carried on among the teachers and custodians as vigorously as among the students. A complete medical examination should be a prerequisite to a position in any educational institution. It is of particular importance to inspect carefully for signs of tuberculosis. The school personnel must be closely supervised during any illness and should be prevented from coming into contact with the students as long as there is danger to them.

Excuses

The problem of excuses arises chiefly in connection with physical education classes. A written excuse by a physician should be the customary method of excusing students from classes. Whenever possible, the school physician should be the only individual authorized to grant excuses. Many unjustifiable excuses have been requested by family physicians. In order to reduce unwarranted excuses to a minimum, the family physician should be requested to write out the reasons why the students should be excused. The school physician should then review the validity of the excuse and in case of doubt require the family physician to prove his point.

When family physicians know that their excuses are subject to the approval of the school physician, they will hesitate to grant unjustifiable excuses. Whenever excuses are granted, their duration should be indicated. When the problem of excuses develops the cause may be that the program is so poor that it does not deserve the support of the physician. Another reason may be that many physicians do not understand the nature and purposes of the program. If this situation prevails it should be rectified. The physicians can be readily approached through the local medical society. The orientation of the physicians should preferably be made by the school medical adviser if one is available.

Additional Health Service Activities

The administration of the school lunch is an important responsibility of the school health service in high schools. The school lunch provides a splendid opportunity to teach and inculcate proper habits as well as to supervise the diets of students suffering from malnutrition. The granting of work permits by the school physician is another health service measure which should be carried out in the high schools. Such a procedure is necessary to prevent students from undertaking more than is good for their health All colleges and universities should provide adequate medical service for their students.

This is the only satisfactory method of assuring proper medical care for students who are away from home. The parents need assurance that their sons and daughters will be properly cared for in illnesses. The student health service and infirmary care should be definitely provided by all colleges, but the best opinion is agreed that strictly therapeutic work should be referred to physicians and specialists practising in the community. The average cost of student health service in colleges is $14.00 a year. This expenses is usually met through student fees and extra charges for special services.

HEALTH INSTRUCTION

Meaning and Purpose of Health Instruction

The third phase of the school health program is health instruction. This term means what it implies, namely, instruction in health. Students learn a great deal about health from the health service and healthful school living phases of health education, but the term health instruction is used to define the effort to promote understanding of health and the observance of desirable health practices. The fundamental purpose of health instruction is to equip the student with sufficient knowledge about health to enable him to attain and maintain, both in attitude and practice, the highest possible level of health.

Importance of Health Instruction

Health instruction is an important means of bringing about healthful behaviour among all people. A healthful environment and excellent health service in themselves will not solve all our health problems. Every individual must make countless decisions which affect not only his own health but the health of others bout him. Many health objectives depend upon the understanding co-operation of all people. Thus, every individual should be capable of intelligent self-direction in matters related to personal and community hygiene. As far as possible everyone should possess a scientific attitude toward health and conduct himself in accordance with recognized scientific knowledge. Ignorance, indifference, and prejudice need to be combated as vigorously as sickness and disease.

The outstanding problem in the prevention of disease at the present time is not the accumulation of more knowledge about disease but the putting into practice of the now available knowledge of disease prevention and control. The failure of many people to employ immunization procedures is an example. Many physical defects developing during childhood, such as those involving hearing, sight, posture, nutrition, including dental decay, could be prevented in large part by intelligent health behaviour. A scientific attitude toward health is needed to break down superstitions and fads and to counteract the misleading advertisements in newspapers, in magazines, and over the radio and television.

The Health Teacher

According to the definition given of health

instruction, this term is to be used to define that time and effort given in class to promote and understanding of health and the practice of health habits. Obviously, in a broader sense, the child learns of health through other classes. In this sense, health instruction is a responsibility of the entire faculty. The health instruction in the elementary school grades is usually considered as best left with the regular grade teacher. She should be as well prepared for this task as she is prepared for arithmetic, reading, or any other subject which she teaches.

This is not usually the case, although in some states certification requirements insure adequate preparation. The junior and senior high school teacher should be especially trained for this particular subject. The practice of having the coach or physical education teacher teach this course is to be condemned unless he has had special preparation. The physician who does not have an education background is likewise unprepared to teach health. Special training in anatomy, physiology, hygiene, health education, bacteriology, psychology, mental hygiene, educational psychology, and teaching methods is recommended. Many times in the small school no faculty members has received such training. This condition requires the selection of the best prepared individual for the position.

In some schools it may be the general science teacher, the physical educator, or the school nurse. Care must be taken to select a teacher who is interested not only in his particular field but in teaching health. Unless the teacher has enthusiasm for his subject, he will be, at very best, a mediocre teacher. Inasmuch as in health instruction there should be a correlation of this subject material with the other subjects in the curriculum the health teacher not only should have had additional preparation but must have a certain amount of co-operativeness, a pleasant personality, and administrative ability in order that these necessary correlations may be made without conflict between faculty members or departments.

Time Allotment

In the first three grades the teaching of health is carried out largely through a correlation of health with the other subjects in the curriculum. However, an average of at lease two periods per week should definitely be devoted to health instruction. In the upper elementary grades this correlation is continued, but, in addition, three periods a week should be devoted specifically to this subject. Specific health course should be required in the secondary school with a minimum time allotment of a daily period for one semester either in the ninth or tenth grade and a similar amount of time in the eleventh or twelfth grade. Six semester hours have been recommended by the National Conference on College Hygiene as the ideal time allotment for colleges and universities. The minimum time devoted to health school not be less than two or three semester hours. Most institutions of higher education require such a course. Many school are not giving proper emphasis to health instruction.

One of the most pernicious practices is to use part of the time allotted to physical education for health instruction. This is sometimes done when inclement weather prevents outdoor physical education activities. In some schools one period per week of the physical education time is given over to health instruction. Other schools do not have a specific time allotment but attempt to teach this subject entirely through the use of special speakers. The speakers mostly used are physicians, dentists, nurses, or public health personnel. Although these talks may have value, health instruction, if it is to take its rightful place in the school program, should be made part of the regular curriculum with a specially prepared teacher in charge.

Basic Principles of Health Instruction

Anderson has recommended the following basic principles, which are recognized as fundamental to sound, effective health instruction:

1. Health work in the school cannot be fully effective unless integrated with the life of the home and the community and the forces in both which can contribute to the child's education.

2. Accompanying, incidental learning always takes place, and teachers should be alert for opportunities to make each learning experience yield greater returns in learning.

3. Each child is unique, learns at his own rate and in his own way, and thus a variety of activities and materials is essential.

4. Repetition, or drill, is justified when the learning must be precise and is useful as a tool or skill.

5. Integrated learning is most effective, and only as it becomes unified, will learning be lasting. Both fragmented learning and isolated facts are ineffective and soon forgotten.

6. Learners should be helped in making

generalizations and in applying these generalizations to various new experiences.

7. Learning experiences are most effective when the child sees the relationship of one experience to the whole of experience.

8. Instructional activities must always be related to the actual experiences of the learners.

9. The objectives of any activity must be specified in terms of learner outcomes and must be recognized as personal goals by the child if learning is to be effective.

10. Emphasis is on the positive aspect of health, not the negative aspects. That is, the aim is to build up and maintain as high a level of health as possible in each child.

11. Health is an end to be gained, not an academic subject.

12. Instruction is directed to the well, or normal, child. Children temporarily below par will be benefited by health practices acquired by the hole class.

13. Throughout school life, health promotion should be one of the objectives of the whole school program.

14. Learning experiences must be adapted to the physiological, psychological, and social development of the children.

15. Instruction must be based on the child's interests, needs, abilities, and backgrounds.

16. Learning results from experience, and opportunities must be provided for experience through participation, doing things, and reacting to situations.

17. Problem-solving provides the most effective learning situation but only when the problems are really and meaningful to the learner.

Scope of Health Instruction Program.

The health instruction program should not be thought of as being limited to the formal health course. Two other aspects of health instruction are recognized as important. These are the incidental instruction and the correlated teaching. The incidental health instruction is that which arises naturally in various contacts with students. In such associations situations develop which enable the instructor to give guidance relative to health matters. The student may come to the physical educator with a personal health problem about which he solicites advice. As result of his close, informal relationship with students the physical education teacher frequently discovers students who need health advice. The report of each student' medical examination provides an exceptionally good opportunity for incidental health instruction.

Correlation. Interest can be aroused an health habits motivated by the ways in which health is taught. In addition to being taught in a definite course devoted to the subject, health school be presented in all of the other school subjects. When health should be presented in all of the other school subjects. When health is taught daily in connection with the sciences, the social studies, physical education, and other fields, with definite objectives to achieve and precise content to cover, the process is known as correlation. The practice of teaching various aspects of health in other school subjects has been long advocated by leaders in the field of health education. In addition to the value of increases interest, it presents an opportunity to bring out essential health information in what might be a more natural setting and thus give the student a better understanding and appreciation of it.

If the faculty member directly responsible for the health program is well trained and is given proper co-operation by the entire teaching staff, a large amount of factual health knowledge can be presented through established subjects in the curriculum. Health instruction is to be looked upon not as a responsibility of the health teachers alone but as a joint responsibility of the entire faculty. Too many times no practical application to the field of health is made by the other teachers. In the junior and senior high school the health co-ordinator is usually responsible for the direct instruction if there is a separate time allotment and for the integration of health with the other subjects in the curriculum.

In colleges and universities the health administrator or health co-ordinator is responsible for the correlations, but he may assign this task to one of his assistants. There are obvious criticisms of the attempt to teach health only through this correlation method. The courses with which health is chiefly correlation may not be elected by the student. The general science teacher, the home economics teacher, and other instructors are interested chiefly in their subject and may not be particularly interested in emphasizing the material relating to health.

The health co-ordinator should be able to show the various other members of the faculty how these correlations can be made in perfectly normal way, and the program should be worked out so that duplication of factual material be minimized as far as possible.

The health course. On the junior and senior high school levels and in colleges and universities formal courses in health are essential. Even though some health may be effectively taught through incidental and correlated instruction, invariably important areas will be omitted. In addition, such a course is needed to provide students with a unified, integrated presentation of the health materials which are related to their needs.

Health instruction in the elementary school. In the elementary grades, health instruction is the responsibility of the classroom teacher. In the primary grades a daily period of health instruction is not essential, but a minimal time allotment would be two 30-minute periods per week. In the intermediate grades three periods of substantial length are needed. It should be stressed that incidental and correlated instruction, of which there is a good deal in the elementary grades, should be over and beyond this time allotment. Another important consideration is that teachable moments arise the teacher may spend considerably more time on health instruction than usual. In the elementary grades, the emphasis is placed upon the development of desirable habits and attitudes toward healthful living.

The scientific facts upon which habits and attitudes are based should not stressed. The instruction should be informal and should grow out of the daily experiences of children. The methods of instruction include discussion, projects, exhibits, demonstrations, construction, oral reports, dramatization, and field trips. A number of studies have provided insight into the health needs and interests of elementary school children. These indicate that the major emphasis in the primary grades should be given to such aspects as developing habits of personal cleanliness; caring for teeth, eyes, ears, and nose; proper eating habits and choice of foods; developing proper attitudes toward physical and dental examinations; preventing colds, skin disease, and other infections; wearing appropriate clothing; and acquiring habits of safety. In the intermediate grades instruction can be continued on many of the above items but on a more advanced level. Other aspects which maybe covered include prevention of infections; nutrition; fire prevention; traffic safety; safety measures in school, home, and playground; rest; getting along with adults; simple first-aid procedures; and purification of water and milk.

Health instruction in the secondary school. In the secondary schools, an increasing emphasis should be given to health knowledge. The development of proper health habits, attitudes, and knowledge should proceed concurrently. Experience has clearly shown that the relationship between health knowledge and health behaviour is not high. Most people with unhealthy habits really know better.

The problem is one of proper attitudes. The correct feelings and emotions must be taught along with the health materials can guide the learning experience so that the feeling and ideas become appropriately associated in the learner. When satisfaction accompanies proper behaviour and dissatisfaction the improper behaviour, correct attitudes will be developed, particularly if the satisfaction and dissatisfaction come immediately. A number of studies of health interests of secondary school students have been made.

In a study of interests of high school boys in the Denver public schools the items of least interest included:

1. Studying about health helpers in the community.

2. Hearing a talk by a nurse on how to take care of the sick.

3. Drawing a diagram showing the structure of tooth.

4. Making a list of safety rules.

5. Making posters of food found in a well-balanced diet.

6. Listening to talks on vitamins.

7. Learning the names of the bones of the body.

Methods of Teaching Health

One of the most common criticisms of health teaching is that the subject lacks interest. This criticism has been made by elementary, and junior and senior high school groups as well as by freshmen in college. It has been due, no doubt, in the past in large part to insufficient training of the health instructor and too much duplication of teaching material. Many school principals, superintendent, and other faculty members still think of health in terms of washing the hands before eating, brushing the teeth three times a day, and drinking six or eight glasses of water daily. Although some of these facts have some value, one can hardly expect interest if they are taught in the elementary grades and again in the junior and senior high school and college. If the health course is to appeal to students, their interests and needs must be considered in the selection of subject matter. These needs and interests are constantly changing; and unless the health instruction is modified and adapted to them and the different school levels, this subject will always prove distasteful and uninteresting.

There is also the tendency to base the instruction predominantly on adult needs and interests. While these are important, it is extremely difficult to interest students in health problems which are thirty to forty years away. The best procedure is to follow the middle path and to consider both present and future needs and interests. In the past of lecture was used predominantly in health education courses, but the trend at present seems to be a combination of the lecture and textbook methods. The use of the textbook is a highly desirable method of teaching hygiene, for it results in greater student activity and application. One of the drawbacks to using a textbook has been the scarcity in the past of good publications in this field. Health texts not only must be well written, interesting, and nontechnical, but they must include the latest developments in all phases of health.

There are constant changes occurring in the subject matter covered in health education, and regardless of how good a book may be today, it may be out of date soon. Fortunately, there are available at present a number of excellent publications, and with the increased interest in this field it appears likely that there will be no lack of good health textbooks in the future. Through the use of well-selected health films, slides, and posters an otherwise uninteresting health course may be made interesting and certainly much more valuable. There are health films available at the present time for elementary, junior, and senior high schools presenting material in an interesting way and including material that many times would be impossible or at least very difficult to present by ordinary class methods.

Health films and slides, however, are not to be looked upon as a teaching method but as a teaching aid. Most of the large college and universities have a visual education unit by which these films and projectors are made available to schools throughout the state by payment of a small rental fee. Slides are available from the same source. The teacher sufficiently interested, with a small amount of training and very little material, should be able to make his or her own collection of slides. Posters are available from most of the national associations, such as The national Safety Council, the National Tuberculosis Association, the National Society of the Prevention of Blindness, or the National Society for the Control of Cancer.

The materials presented by these associations are authentic, and the teacher should not neglect these sources. The use of class demonstrations is a very effective means of presenting health facts. The teacher should have received sufficient training in health so that various simple experiments may be carried out. The growth requirements of bacteria, their wide distribution, the effects of drying, sunlight, boiling, and pasteurization on them can be easily demonstrated. A comparison can be made of the bacterial count of raw milk with that of pasteurized milk or of river water with tap water.

The size and the shape of various types of bacteria can be easily shown by the staining of these organisms and by the use of the microscope. Simple feeding experiments carried out as a class project would be an interesting and worthwhile method of presenting certain facts in this field. There are many other simple, inexpensive demonstrations which may be made. There are on the market various health workbooks and laboratory guides which should be of value to the teacher for class demonstrations. In every community there are various class trips that can be taken which should add interest and value to health instruction.

A visit to the sewage-disposal and water plants will create more interest in municipal health problems than will ordinary classroom instruction. A visit to some good dairy to show modern sanitary methods of processing milk and to a farm where precautions are not taken should be interesting and valuable. The health teacher should take every opportunity of utilizing those facilities available in the community. Some universities and colleges are able to use human cadavers and specimens to facilitate instruction. In junior and senior high schools an excellent device is to put on a health exhibit.

Safeguarding Health

All teacher are responsible for protecting the health of the school population. The physical education teacher's obligations in this regard are more difficult to discharge, however. In the service, intramural, and interschool programs there are many potential hazards to the health of students. Adoption of the following policies would do much to elimination such dangers.

1. A medical examination should be a prerequisite to participation. No student should be permitted to participate in the physical education program unless his physical status permits it. An annual medical examination is a necessity for all students participating

in the interschool athletic program. A school medical examination within three years should be a prerequisite for participation in the service and intramural programs. It is recommended that the hearts of intramural participants be checked each year. Intramural activities are often very strenuous, and the greatest danger is to the heart. This phase of the medical examination would be relatively simple to administer.

2. Proper physical conditioning should precede intensive participation. Intensive participation in physical education activities should be preceded by a gradual, progressive physical conditioning program. This is particularly important in the interschool program but applies also to the intramural and service programs. This policy has been most frequently violated in intramural athletics.

3. A physician should be in attendance at all football games, wrestling meets, and other contests which have a high incidence of injuries. If this is not possible, arrangements should be made whereby he could be reached quickly.

4. An adequate worm-up should precede all participation in vigorous sports and games. Many injuries are caused by the failure to observe this precaution.

5. Medical approval should be required for participation after illness or injury. A student who has been absent from school because of serious illness or injury should, before he resumes participation, present a statement from a doctor which indicates that he is physically fit to participate.

6. Competition should be arranged between teams

and individuals of comparable ability. This is particularly important for competition in the rugged body-contact sports where the possibility of injury is greatest. This policy applies equally well to competition in the service and intramural as in the interschool program.

7. Interscholastic boxing should be prohibited. The American Association for Health, Physical Education, and Recreation and the Joint Committee on Health Problems in Education of the National Education Association and the American Medical Association have gone on record as opposed to interscholastic boxing. Boxing is an extremely hazardous activity and its dangers are out of proportion to its possible benefits. Blows to the head may cause injury to the centres of the brain that regulate memory, speech, self-control, and the power of reasoning which can result in loss in mental power and physical co-ordination. Such injuries may occur to novice in his first contest or to an experienced boxer. They may occur without a "knockout" or a skull fracture.

8. Equipment and facilities should be maintained in a safe condition. Slippery floors, extraneous objects on the floor, uneven playing surfaces, unsafe equipment, and equipment which does not provide adequate protection are all common causes of injury.

9. Capable officiating should be provided. Incompetent officiating is recognized as one of most important causes of injury in athletic competition.

10. Unsanitary practices should be eliminated. Many unsanitary practices are permitted in physical education, particularly in interscholastic athletics. The common water bottle, towel, or sponge is still frequently

used. The practice of sliding a towel across the floor is not uncommon. Athletic clothing is interchanged among students. Clean equipment is not required. The practice of expectorating on the floor is not prohibited. In some schools, shower facilities are not available. The continuance of such practices is a denial of health as a physical education objective.

11. Special provision should be made for students who have physical disabilities which prevent them from participating in the regular program. These students should be assigned to remedial classes or to classes in modified activity. Such handicapped individuals are in greater need of physical education than normal students.

12. Activities should not overtax the physical capacities of immature students. Physical education activities which place a heavy demand upon endurance are contraindicated for elementary and junior high school students.

13. Students must be protected from constant failure and too much easy success in physical education activities. The physical educator must protect the student from injury to this personality and emotional adjustment just as much as he must protect him from physical injury. He should help student recognize their powers and limitations. He must watch that no student withdraws into himself too much. He should see that everyone is a member of a group—that no one is rejected continuously.

14. Adequate medical and hospital care should be provided for injured athletes. In many schools such medical care is paid for by the school or is covered by

insurance. Ideally, such coverage should also be provided for students injured in the instructional and intramural programs. However, few schools can afford such a service.

15. Suitable protective equipment should be provided every participant. Many injuries in physical education are due to inadequate protective equipment. This is particularly true in rugged, contact sorts, such as football, soccer, lacrosse, rugby, ice hockey, and wrestling.

10

Motor Learning and Teaching Methods

Learning may be considered to be a more or less permanent change in performance associated with experiences but excluding changes which occur through maturation and degeneration, or through alterations in the receptor or effector organs.

Performance may be thought of as a temporary occurrence. Fluctuating from time to time because of many potentially operating variables. We usually use performance to represent the amount of learning that has occurred, for the process of learning must be inferred on the basis of observations of change in performance.

Learning is considered to be the commitment of skills and knowledge to memory. We discussed, input, which can also be termed stimulus, and how this is processed to produce an appropriate output or response. We saw that this process requires that we view what is to be learned as relevant, that we are attentive to what we are doing and that we are prepared to practise so that the information or movement becomes grooved in memory. In this section we will consider three important general theories of learning:

—associationist theory

—cognitive theory

—social learning theory.

Firstly, however, a word of warning. Much of what we know about motor learning derives from laboratory experiments. They have been well constructed and the methods used are reliable and valid, because experiments are able to control variables that cannot be easily controlled in a real-life situation. What is often not clear, however, is (i) how permanent the observed improvements in performance are and (ii) whether observed learning in the laboratory can be transferred to sport situations. Bear this in mind when your further reading introduces you to actual experiments and in particular if you devise your own for a project. Another thing to remember as you read this section is that the most important factor to influence learning is the amount of practice the player has.

To maximise learning and performance, maximise practice. But, there are two kinds of practice: (i) that which occurs through participation in the sport or activity the game, the tournament, the dance, performance, the expedition; (ii) what Ericsson calls deliberate practice, i.e., activities designed by the coach to improve specific aspects of performance. We all know that this kind of practice requires effort and is not always enjoyable and teachers about how to structure motor learning runs the underlying maxim that motivation must be maintained and practice, if now always enjoyable, must be satisfying. Before moving to the main learning theories, we will study a model of learning which links closely with the information-processing approach.

Phases of Motor Learning

We know that people learn at different rates and have different preferred ways of learning; good coaching takes account of these differences. It is clear also that the coaching needs of an expert are different from those of a novice. Fitts and Posner suggest that this progression from novice to expert can be modelled using information-processing concepts. Their model helps coaches to analyse what stage of learning their athlete are at and structure practice accordingly.

Cognitive (Early) Phase

The learner tries to get to grips with the nature of the activity to be learned, to figure out what to do. Demonstrations are important, but so are verbal explanations to highlight the important cues. Problem solving also seems to work in the prepractice stage. The learner tries to memorise sequences of movements and it often helps to verbalise these. Teachers must be aware that information overload is a danger at this stage, because the learners have to think about almost every element of the action as they practise it and may have to visually focus on the movement as well as the area of play or performance. Teachers should also bear in mind that many learners want to get on with it and have a go. Feedback should focus on the reinforcement of correct responses and on shaping. Performance is full of errors and movement is inconsistent and lacks fluency. 'Trial and Error' learning interspersed with feedback and instruction will fulfil most learner's needs.

Associative (Intermediate) Phase

The learner now understands the aim of the activity. Movement patterns are now more fluent and integrated. Simple aspects of the skill are becoming well learned and there is scope to refine the more complex aspects. The aim of the learner is to begin to associate the feel of the movements with the end results. Feedback should be specific and focus on both knowledge of performance and knowledge of results to allow the association of kinesthetic feedback with outcomes.

Autonomous (Final) Phase

Movement patterns are now well integrated and automatic; they can be performed without the performer giving conscious attention to the movement, unless it is required. The performer can concentrate on the external demands of the environment and give a lot of attention to subtle cues. For example, a tennis player can use the opponent's wrist and racket action to judge what kind of spin is being put on to the ball, a task impossible for a novice because there is too much else to think about.

There is less need for feedback from the teacher, because the performers are able to judge their own performances, but any information feedback can now be very detailed and specific. The rate at which a learner progresses through the phases is determined by practice, effectiveness of information processing and the nature and extent of the reinforcement, guidance and feedback available.

Association (Stimulus-Response) Theories

This group of theories are all about the relationship between a stimulus and the response. Learning is said to have occurred when the presentation of the *stimulus* usually produces an appropriate *response*. The more stimulus and response occur close together in practice, the more the *S-R bond* is established in the memory and strengthened. Early psychologists focused on the automatic nature of this bond.

Classical Conditioning

This is a basic form of S-R learning. It was studied by Pavlov, an eminent Russian physiologist, who used dogs as his subjects. In a controlled experiment, he presented food to a hungry dog, first ringing a bell a few seconds before giving the food. The smell and/or sight of food causes dogs to salivate automatically, as a reflex. At first, the bell had no effect on the dog, but within a few trials the dog started to associate the sound of the bell with food and began to salivate as soon as the bell sounded, even before the food was produced. It is important to recognise what has been learned in this example—not new behaviour but to behave in the same way to a new stimulus through association of the first stimulus with the second. Humans can learn through classical conditioning. For example, if a puff of air is blown into someone's eye to make them blink and this stimulus is paired with a bell, the person soon learns to blink when they hear the bell. But human reflexes are limited in number.

Most of our learning depends on developing new responses and skills, not on association with innate, unconscious reflexes. Some writers refer to learned reflexes i.e., movements which have been learned but which are not under conscious control. Withdrawing your hand from a hot surface or ducking if something is thrown near your head are two examples. If we accept this notion, we can extend the range of behaviours which we could claim to be classically conditioned. We could learn irrational fear responses by this form of conditioning. This might explain some children's fear in a swimming pool. But it is still an association between two stimuli which is being conditioned, not the behaviour. As physical educationalists or sport scientists, it is the behaviour we are interested in. So where do completely new skills, for example, performing a somersault, come from?

Operand (Instrumental) Conditioning

Skinner suggests that, even though much of our behaviour is not reflexive, it can still be conditioned, but not by classic methods. Naturally, occurring, learned behaviour is called *operant* behaviour. If this behaviour is rewarded in some way, then there is an increased likelihood of it occurring again; we seem to be programmed to seek reward of satisfaction. A young swimmer is learning a tumble turn. The first attempts at the somersault are not successful but sooner or later, perhaps accidentally, his or her feet touch the wall and the push-off is effective. This is a good feeling, particularly if the coach gives the praise and encouragement. This satisfaction acts as a *positive reinforcer*. It strengthens the connection between the stimulus and the response. Positive reinforcement is a relatively straightforward concept.

Feelings of satisfaction can be generated by the outcome of the response, or can be given the teacher in the form of praise. Negative reinforcement is rather more difficult to understand. Look again at the definition again; an example may help. The coach has been working with the soccer team on some defensive drills. The team has been working hard but is keen to put the drills into a real game. The coach is trying to set up a conditioned game but the players are anticipating the excitement of competition and are not paying attention. The coach wants them to listen. He stops the explanation, waits for attention and says, 'Until you stands still and listen to what we are going to do, we are not going to start. It is your playing time we are wasting'. Not allowing the coaching session to continue is the negative reinforcement; it is unpleasant because the team are keen to play.

Playing attention to the coach is the required response. Once the team are doing so, the negative reinforcement is removed, i.e., the coach stops holding up the game. Hopefully, the players learn that if they want to have plenty of time in the game they must listen to the coach. It is important not to confuse negative reinforcement with punishment. Punishment is given as a *consequence* of a response and to prevent the response occurring again. To extend the example, if one of team continued to mess about the coach might say, 'I have worned you once. You are still not doing what I asked, so you are not going to play for the first 10 minutes. Go and get your tracksuit on'. The punishment of not playing is designed to stop Sam misbehacing in future. Skinner extended his theory of operant conditioning to include the concept of *shaping*. He recognised that with complex skills, for example a tennis serve, you cannot immediately reinforce the whole action because it is unlikely to be produced in the first trial. So the coach might:

—break the skill down into small, easily learned parts and progressively reinforce these, building the whole skill up; this is sometimes called *chaining*

—or introduce the whole skill, but shape it by reinforcing actions which are along the right lines, even if not quite right. By reinforcing actions which are closer and closer approximations to the desired end result, the overall correct movement is gradually learned.

Operant conditioning facilitates the initial learning of the skill. Once a skill is learned, there is no need to continue reinforcement and so it can be gradually withdrawn and transferred to the learning of a more advanced skill. As long as this withdrawal does not happen before the skill is learned, the S-R bond will not be weakened.

Thorndike's Laws of Learning

Thorndike was an extremely influential S-R theorist. He established three laws of learning which are particularly important in skill development.

Law of Readiness

Learning can only take place when the nervous system is sufficiently mature to allow the appropriate S-R connections. Basic body management skills, such as jumping, running, skipping, should be developed before the implementation of striking and catching skills. This concept of nervous system and readiness is in addition to issues of muscle strength and skeletal maturity, which are also very important considerations.

Law of Effect

Learning occurs when a particular response has an effect on the person, i.e., when the response is reinforced. Satisfying reinforcers increase the strength of the S-R bond and increase the likelihood of the response being repeated. Thus, to enable early success it is important for a coach or teacher to use positive feedback to reinforce correct attempts. If the learner knows what he or she is trying to achieve, then observed success can serve as a positive reinforcer and failures as a punishment, without a teacher or coach being there to provide supplementary reinforcement. This process has become known as trial and error learning. It depends on the learner being able to recognise success and to feel satisfaction with the response or alternatively to admit that a response is not appropriate and to try another. The problem of this approach to skill learning is that it can allow learners to establish bad habits, i.e., responses that are immediately successful at the beginner stage but that do not allow further development.

Law of Exercise

Repetition strengthens the S-R bond, hence the importance of practice. Even though a skill may have apparently been learned effectively, practice beyond this point leads to mastery learning. Mastery learning ensures that a skill is not easily forgotten and can be performed under varied and difficult circumstances.

Cognitive Theories

S-R theory has been very influential in helping us to understand how people become skilful but many psychologists, particularly today, do not believe it is the whole answer. They argue that the extent, variety and richness of human learning cannot be explained solely by S-R bonding. A number of alternative theories, known as *cognitive* theories, have been put forward. These are called cognitive because they place a greater emphasis on thought processes and on understanding how concepts relate to one another than is evident in S-R theory. Tolman believed that behaviour is driven by purpose and expectation, so learners are motivated to work towards goals of which they are aware.

In sport and PE these are the skills and understandings which make up the particular activity. Learners progress towards the goal by recognising cues, using past experience and forming what Tolman referred to as a *cognitive map* of the activity, which becomes more complex and sophisticated as the learner becomes more skilful. A group of psychologists known as the *Gestaltists* proposed two principles of learning:

i. Learning can be accelerated by using insight or intuition to solve a problem. For example, a gymnast and her coach might want to link two moves in floor sequence but are not sure how to do it. The gymnast may experiment with several ideas which help to clarify the problems and possibilities and might then suddenly say, 'I known, how about' and produce the movement solution—a moment of insight.

ii. Learning is most effective when a problem is seen as a whole or when the whole pattern of a movement can be practised. This enables the learner to understand all the issues and relationships which need to be considered.

Gestaltists therefore advocate that learners practise a tennis serve as a whole, without breaking it down into parts.

Social (Observational) Learning Theory

Social learning theory explains how our behaviour is influenced by the behaviour of other people. Coaches and teachers are using this theory when they employ demonstration as a learning tool. Demonstration is a powerful teaching tool in skill acquisition. Youngsters are involved in observational learning when they copy sporting heroes. Demonstration is the application of modelling or observational learning. This theory maintains that much social behaviour is learned through observation of models and skilled behaviour is no exception to this.

One problem of observational learning is that teachers and coaches cannot always control what players are learning. A youngster might learn a lot about skill from watching his football hero but he may also pick up some bad habits too. Bandura suggests that there are four processes in observational learning:

i. attention and retention, which relate to the acquisition of the skill

ii. motor reproduction and motivation, determining performance

iii. coaches and teachers use this model when they demand that players attend to instructions or provide cues about how best to perform

iv. retention is the process of remembering the modelled behaviour. Good coaches helps this process by repetition, by making learning interesting by encouraging mental imagination of the skill and by catchprases step-step-step-lift, helps the hurdle step in springboard diving.

—Motor reproduction refers to the attempt by the learner at the modelled skill. It is important that the coach has demonstrated correctly and also that the learner has the physical make-up to be able to do the task. Further guidance is usually helpful at this stage.

—People tend to imitate what they are interested in and motivated to achieve. Good coaches understand what motivates their players and use this as an important coaching tool. They use reinforcement to enhance motivation.

Motivation and Drive Theory

The topic of motivation occurs throughout the theory and practice of teaching and learning. To achieve anything, we need to be motivated. Hull defines learning in terms of motivation; he suggests that whenever we have need to learn, this sets up a psychological drive to satisfy that need. This is in turn leads to an action or response. If this is successful, then the drive is reduced and motivation will only be maintained if a new need to learn arises or is presented to us. This is a very complex theory in its totality but stated simply and applied to physical activity, it suggests that as a movement problem arises, for example, in dance choreography or the performance of a particular skill in a game, this generates a need for competence, a need to solve the problem.

This need in turn develops a drive and an incentive to learn to solve the problem and also a habit. So we start to practise. At first the performance is not effective but as success comes it is perceived as a reward and thus acts as reinforcement. As a result a memory bond if forged between the stimulus and the response is developed. As our performance improves, so the habit is strengthened and the drive to go on learning reduced. At this point the teacher or coach needs to extend the problem or present a new one to maintain interest and motivation. The coach also needs to be aware of the Hull called inhibition. This is a phenomena we have probably all noticed, that during a long practice session our performance may be less good at the end than it was earlier in the session. This does not mean, however, that we are not learning throughout the session, what is evident at the end of practice may not be what is retained or what is transferred into the competitive or performance environment. Developing motivational strategies as a teacher or learner can be complex; we all know how difficult it is to motivate ourselves to do something we are not to keen on.

To be successful, coaches need to be aware of just

what motivates their players and how to get the best out of them. This seems to be a major determinant in the success of British professional football managers. Schmidt states the problem very simply; to him motivation consists of:

making the task seem important

goal setting.

Feedback

Feedback is sensory information that results from movement. You will find several different terms to define it. We can simply matters if we focus on the feedback as it is consciously used by the learner and coach. Schmidt names two forms, inherent feedback and augmented feedback.

i. Inherent Feedback: It derives from the performance of the skill itself. It is information about the muscles involved, the coordination and timing of the movement, the effectiveness and the outcome. It is used for error detection as the movement is in progress, by the comparison of movement as it progresses with the model stored in memory. It is also used for reinforcement: a javelin thrower might know that the throw felt good but waits in anticipation of the javelin coming back to earth to see if the throw is as long as he feels it is. Both are examples of inherent feedback.

ii. Augmented Feedback: It is information provided about the task which is in addition to that provided as a direct result of the movement. It might be provided by an official, a coach, a video, a results board or team mate. There are several dimensions to augmented feedback. These dimensions should be thought of as independent of each other. The dimensions defines the most forms of feedback used. Being aware of them helps the coach to decide how best to provide feedback in a particular set of circumstances.

Functions of Feedback

Feedback has four functions:

i. Information about performance or outcome

ii. Reinforcement

iii. Punishment

iv. Motivation

i. Feedback for information

Information feedback can be either inherent or augmented. Augmented feedback should be structured by the teacher or coach such that it gives (i) reinforcement of correct performance and (ii) help with correcting errors. It should include:

—the outcome of the performance

—correct and incorrect aspects

—what the correct movement response should feel like

—explanation of the cause of errors

—changes in technique or tactics to correct the errors

—why these changes are suggested.

The good coach gives positive information feedback first, followed by error correction and finally some motivational comment. Before giving feedback, the coach also gives the learner a moment or two to evaluate and come to conclusions about his or her own performance. Sometimes questions can be used: 'What did that feel like?' 'Why do you think that happened?'. This gives control to the learner, identifies to the coach the ability of the learner to analyse his or her own performance and ensures the coach does not tell the learner what he or she already knows. For beginners, information feedback should be simple and concise.

It should focus on sequence and timing so that the motor programme can be developed effectively. It should be given as frequently as possible, after each trial if feasible; it should help the learner identify important cues; it should rely on visual and verbal input. For intermediate learners, feedback can be given less frequently, the learner needs opportunity to link the feel of the movement with the outcomes, so information feedback should focus on this. The feedback can be more detailed. Advanced performers require much less, augmented information feedback; what is given should be detailed and technical.

ii. Feedback for Reinforcement

Reinforcement is used a great deal in the early learning stages and through all the phases for open skills. It can be intrinsic or augmented. Positive reinforcement is given to strengthen the desired technique. It can be used to shape responses. In sports contexts positive reinforcement usually takes the form of praise and encouragement. Augmented negative reinforcement requires the removal of an unpleasant consequences of the error. For example, there is a device which a golfer may attach to his or her club that gives a loud click if the golfer snatches the swing.

Negative reinforcement is the avoidance of the click by swinging smoothly. Practising allows negative reinforcement to eliminate the error and reinforce the correct swing. Reinforcement must be given immediately following the response if it is to be effective.

Feedback as Punishment

Coaches and teachers ideally should not need to punish, but players are not angels and occasionally misbehaving or refuse to accept a coach's or teacher's advice. Punishment carries risks and should be used sparingly and only if all other forms of feedback appear to be ineffective. An example of punishment is to demote a player to the bench for a game for missing a practice.

Punishment should not:

—be physical or involve physical activity

—demean the learner or damage their self-esteem

—be given in frustration or anger.

Punishment should:

—be perceived as such by the learner

—be given after warning

—be used consistently and fairly

—be used against the undesirable behaviour, not the person

—be supplemented by positive reinforcement and motivational feedback.

Feedback as Motivation

Learners are motivated when they have clear goals and want to believe them. Goal setting in sport is an important element in learning and the good teacher or coach ensures that learners have clear, achievable structured goals to which they are committed. Motivational feedback gives learners information about their progress towards these goals. It helps them to understand the difference between their present performance level and that needed to achieve their goal.

It is important that it also gives them self-belief and the confidence to continue to practise through the ups and downs of learning. Breaking down long-term goals, for example to reach the national championships, into more immediate goals is a helpful motivational strategy.

Progress charts and training or competition diaries are useful in this respect, because they help the learner to see improvement. But often the most satisfying motivational feedback comes as acknowledgement of progress from the teacher or coach.

Transfer of Learning

Schema theory seems to imply that certain aspects of a skill learned in one situation can determine performance in another similar situation. This is named transfer in the skill acquisition literature. Transfer is defined as the effect of the learning and performance of one skill on the learning and performance of another. If this effect is on a skill that is about to be learned it is referred to as proactive transfer. Retroactive transfer occurs on skills already learned. It is important to note that not all transfer enhances learning. Teachers and coaches attempt to use positive transfer whenever possible.

Stallings identifies a variety of forms of transfer in addition to the general categories. Transfer of complex concept and is not easy to apply in the learning-teaching situation. What can we learn from the research literature?

—The greater the actual similarity between skills, the greater the possibility of positive transfer.

—The greater the dissimilarity, the less likelihood exists of positive transfer.

—Where skills share some similarities but have

important differences, there is the danger of negative transfer.

—Athletes learn new techniques and tactics more effectively if new learning builds on and is related to skills already learned.

—Coaches or teachers should emphasise the similarity between the skills when teaching for transfer.

—Tactical understanding can be transferred.

—General principles of attack and defence play can be transferred in invasion games.

—The more thoroughly the first skill has been learned, the more effective is the transfer.

—In activities where bilateral transfer is encouraged, it is important that the skill is well learned on the preferred limb before transfer is attempted to the other.

—Virtual reality-reality transfer: does playing a computer-based game of soccer, for example, improve skill in the real thing? Recent research indicates that knowledge of the procedures of the skill may be enhanced but there is little evidence of transfer of the perceptual and motor elements. Results from an experiment with a table tennis game were more positive.

Let us consider transfer of learning in a broader context by taking the example of a good gymnast who goes to college and follows a beginner's dance course as part of his or her A-level or under-graduate studies. To what extent does successful experience in gymnastics and learning in dance?

Teaching

So far in this chapter we have considered some lements of the learning process. This section focuses on how learning may be structured so that it is achieved efficiently. You should bear these points in mind when planning your own practice or training or when helping others with theirs. We have referred to teaching and coaching as if they are the same activity. Whereas some argue that they have different aims and purposes, current approaches suggest that teaching physical education and coaching sport share much common ground, so we treat them as one process.

The Teaching Process

Most learning is achieved by being taught in one way or another, although 'trial and error' learning or 'learning by experience' also occur. Teaching others is a process we are all involved in, even though we may not consider ourselves to be teachers. Teaching is about giving experiences or advice which aids learning. Current theory suggests there are four elements of the teaching process—instructing, demonstration, applying and confirming—and good teaching progresses through each in turn.

Instructing

In the instructing phase, teachers make sure that learners understand and task and have enough information to allow them to start practising. Usually this is done verbally, though written practice schedules or worksheets are sometimes used. The danger is this phase that the teachers give too much information. Unless the information given is clear and concise, most of it is quickly forgotten.

Demonstration

As we have seen, demonstration is an important aspect of skill learning because of the need for the learner to establish a model of the skill in memory. It needs to be carefully planned so that both teacher and learner are clear about the purpose of the demonstration and what exactly is to be learned from it. A bad demonstration may be worse than no demonstration at all.

Applying

Applying is the opportunity for the learner to practise the skill; without plenty of time for this, effective learning is unlikely to take place. The teacher's role is to structure this practice effectively and by appropriate guidance to help learners to apply what they have learned from instruction and demonstration to the activity itself.

Confirming

Confirming is the feedback process. It is an essential part of the learning process but is sometime omitted by teachers, to the detriment of learning. An important part of reviewing is to question the learner about what he or she has learned and the progress made. This not only helps the teacher to confirm what has been learned, but also encourages the learner to be self-evaluative and reinforcers learning.

Styles of Teaching

Within the four elements of the teaching process described above there are many different ways to teach. These are known as styles and have been analysed and classified in much the same way that we have classified in much the same way that we have classified skill, that is, by observing action, noting the characteristics of that action and devising a theoretical framework to fit the observations. Mosston & Ashworth produced a classification which they have labelled the spectrum of teaching styles. They suggest that teaching and learning are essentially about making decisions: what to teach-learn; when to teach-learn; how to present and acquire the ideas and skills, etc. Their model suggests that at one end of the spectrum the teacher makes all these decisions and at the other end the learner makes them all.

In between are a range of styles in which the teacher and learner are both involved in decision making. The styles are distinct and Mosston & Ashworth give them letter labels and names. It is very difficult to teach for long in command style and it is not advisable to do so, because we usually want to hand some of the decisions to the learners, e.g., start when you are ready. Command style is used when a teacher wants tight control over what the learner is doing or wants uniformity in a class. A lot of aerobics and keep-fit teaching is done in command styles. Another style if practice style—the teacher sets the task but the student work on it in their own time. Another style is known as reciprocal style. Pupils work in pairs—one is the doer and the other the observer. In this style the teacher hands over all contact with the learners to fellow pupils. The teacher makes sure either by a worksheet or by very explicit instructions, that all the pupils understand the task and the criteria for successful completion of it. It is then up to the observer to help the doer; the teacher helps the observer with their teaching. It is a useful style with large groups because it allows each learner a lot of immediate feedback.

Modes of Presentation

Teaching style is concerned with the way in which a teacher opts to deal with the range of decisions that the teaching process imposes. One of these decisions is, 'How do I present this new information or skill to my pupils?' The answer to this question depends on the teacher's analysis of two important factors. Task analysis involves deciding what the important elements of the task are. Information-processing theory helps here.

—What are the perceptual requirements?

—What are the decision-making requirements?

—What techniques does the performer need?

—What feedback is available?

Answers to these questions indicate the complexity of the task. Note that complexity relates to the nature of the task; whether a task is simple or difficult depends upon the amount of attention or processing space that needs to be given to it and the experience of the learner. Analysis should also indicate the extent to which the skill is organised. Skills which are not easily broken down into constituent parts are said to be highly organised. Swimming strokes are examples of low organisation, because the leg, arm and breathing actions are all different and separate, although obviously they need to be well coordinated for effective performance. This task analysis should be compared with an analysis of the state of readiness and the capabilities of the learner. The good teacher and coach consider age, previous experience, physical abilities, preferred learning style, motivation and goals.

Whole Practice

Ideally, a skill should be taught as a whole. The learner can then appreciate the end production and can develop a feeling for the flow of movement necessary for a smooth, efficient production of the skill; he or she can see the relationship between the movements which constitute the whole action.

Part Practice

However, for some skills it is not appropriate or sensible to teach the whole all at once, such as:

—when the skill is too complex and/or difficult for the learner, i.e., a lot of information processing is required

—when there is an element of danger.

In these cases the skill is broken down into its constituent parts; these parts are taught as separate actions and then put together, which can be done in a variety of ways. Part methods of teaching are useful when the skill is complex and/or difficult, not highly organised and the mechanics of the movement are important. Closed skills, such as those in gymnastics, diving and trampolining, are usually taught in this way. It lessens fear and risk in dangerous skills and allows the teacher to focus on key elements of the skill. It may help motivation, as the teacher can structure the teaching of the parts as mini wholes, thus giving the learner a feeling of success and progress.

The main problem is one of transfer, but it is essential that the separately taught elements be practise in the same way as they are performed within the whole skill, which is not easy to achieve. It is also important that the whole skill be demonstrated to the learner initially so that the end product can be appreciated in terms of its purpose, pace, flow and organisation.

11

Class Organization and Planning

The present study deals predominantly with problems and details involved in conducting physical activity classes; however, some of the material applies equally well to academic classes, for the two types have much in common.

Tacking Roll

There is no one method of roll taking that is superior to all others for all occasions; instead, there are several good methods commonly used. Still, some of those most generally employed have little to recommend them. Accuracy, speed, and freedom from additional expense are the three essentials of good roll taking. Student participation and learning to know the students by name are elements vastly more to these two than does roll taking. With this in mind the following common methods are listed, explained, and evaluated.

Recording visible members. The numbers are painted on the floor in one or two lines. Th~ students are assigned members according to height, with the tall ones on the smaller numbers to the instructor's left as he faces the class; the shortest pupil is at the end of the line to the instructor's right on the largest assigned number. The instructor then writes on a small card the numbers that are not covered. These are later recorded in the class book. This is a good method if the class is to meet in the same place each time and the surface is such that the numbers may be placed there permanently. It is accurate and quick, but it does not provide for student participation or for acquainting the instructor with the student, and there is a small additional expense.

Recording by squads. The class is arranged according to height from right to left. The first six or eight men on the right constitute the first squad; the next six or eight constitute the next squad; and so on down the line. The names are placed in the class book in this order. A squad leader and an assistant squad leader are appointed or elected for each squad. Numbers may be assigned to each member of the squads. In taking roll, the instructor says "Squads report!" The squad leaders take one step forward in order and report any absences in their respective squads. The instructor notes on a small card the absent numbers or names and later transfers them to the class book. This method is acceptable, although usually less accurate and slightly more time consuming than the other recommended methods. It involves no additional expenses, provides for student participation and can be used on the playground or in the gymnasium since it is not restricted to any one place.

Recording absent numbers. In this method the students are lined up according to height as above, and each pupil is assigned a number, the tallest receiving number "For taking roll, count!" The instructor watches the class during the count and writes the absent numbers on a small card. The record is transferred to the class book later. This is an excellent method of taking roll; it is accurate, quick, provides for student participation, can be used anywhere, and involves no extra cost. In this method, as in others, it may be well to read the numbers marked absent as a means of checking any error the instructor may have made in recording the numbers.

Calling the roll by names. As the heading implies, the names are read from the class book, and each student answers when named is called. For general purposes throughout a term this is a very poor method, except in those case where the instructor can take roll while the class is warming up. It takes too much time an is not outstandingly accurate; however, it does aid in associating faces with names, provides for some student participation, and involves no extra cost. As a means of learning to pronounce the names and of becoming partially acquainted with the students, it serves a useful purpose for the first few meetings of the class each term. After that it should be replaced by some more rapid method.

Alphabetical plan. The class lines up in alphabetical order. Roll is then taken by names or numbers. After roll has been taken it is necessary for the class to reassemble according to height. This plan requires too much time and provides for added confusion through the necessity of reassembling; hence, it is not to be recommended.

Use of tag board. This takes different forms, but in

general each student is given a tag numbered to correspond to its peg on the board. Roll is checked according to the tags that remain or are missing as the case may be. This method is not to be recommended, for it is not particularly accurate or time saving, and additional expense is involved. If the students keep their tags a part of the time, some are apt to be lost; and if they do not keep them, there is little excuse for providing them.

Planning

One of the most essential problems that is frequently overlooked it that of planning the daily program for each class. This should be done carefully. It is only the novice who needs to write out in detail the various aspects of the lesson to be taught, although capable, experienced teachers can usually profit by jotting down a few brief notes or key words as they think through the coming lesson. An excellent teacher can teach a good lesson on the spur of the moment but can do much better if the lesson is planned ahead. In planning the lesson, the instructor should include those activities and techniques which will provide a positive answer to the following questions:

1. Does the activity fit the facilities?

(a) Are the supplies and equipment adequate and at hand?

(b) Are the playing surfaces satisfactory for the activities?

(c) Is there enough room?

3. Is this plan educationally sound?

(a) Does it fit in well with the lesson that has precede it and the one that is to follow?

(B) Are leadership opportunities for the students provided?

(c) Is it interesting?

Is it seasonal?

Is it graded to the level of the students?

Does it involve natural racial activities in abundance?

(d) Does it provide participation for each student for most of the period?

(e) Are the students reasonably familiar with the rules and techniques of the activities considered?

(g) Do the various parts of the lesson integrate will—that is, can the students move from one part to the next with a minimum of rearrangement of equipment and groups involved?

3. Does the whole lesson constitute a healthful procedure?

(a) Are dangerous activities eliminated?

(b) Are pupils properly dressed for these activities?

(c) Are pupils kept from exercising too hard or too long?

(d) Is the area of action clean and sanitary?

(e) Is the temperature satisfactory?

(f) Are all given stimulating exercise?

Dress and Inspection

A change of clothes for activity periods is not advisable for children in the lower grades in most situations, for the allotted time is too short, the "gym outfit" is hard to provide in many cases, and younger children perspire less freely than do older ones who engage in more sustained exercise. In the more advanced school grades, where uniforms are required, it is the instructor's responsibility to see that they are suited to the activity and that they are kept clean. A class looks much better, morale is easier to maintain, and differences in social status are minimized, if all members are dressed in the same type of uniform; consequently, a common type is recommended. If all are not required to wear the same general type, the instructor should make known the specifications of an acceptable uniform and allow no exception to those specifications. On the high school level the inspection for cleanliness should be periodic, systematic, and quickly done.

If the basket system is used for storing the activity clothes when not in use, a check of the baskets on the days designated as wash days for all pupils will reveal those outfits that have not been taken home. If checking is done in class, the instructor can do this quickly after roll has been taken, noting clothes that need to be washed. Friday, or the last activity class meeting of the week, is a good day for this. Then a further check on Monday, or the next activity class meeting day, will reveal how many have cleaned their clothes. As implied above, an occasional general wash day for high school students for all uniforms should be designated. Enforceable penalties, known beforehand to the students, will need to be applied to those who fail to meet established standards of cleanliness. Rigid enforcement rather than severity of penalties is to be recommended. In college a clean uniform should be required.

Absence and Tardiness

The same general rules that apply to absence and tardiness in other classes in the school should apply to activity classes in physical education. If there are no school rules in regard to these matters, the physical education department should make its own rules. They should be few in number, not extremely severe, but rigidly enforced. Each student should be informed at the beginning of the term or semester concerning attendance regulations and, in addition, reminded once or twice during the term. A minimum of scolding and exhorting coupled with a maximum of enforcing will soon establish ample respect for regulations. If it is generally known that violations cannot be "fixed up," there will be fewer violations.

The instructor's time should be given to those who comply with the regulations rather than wasted in an effort to grant special privileges to those who do not comply. The student who misses class just because he chooses to do so is losing that opportunity and should not be allowed to recall it. Even though it is wise practice to reduce make-up work to the very minimum, justice served better by providing make-up opportunities for those who merit consideration because of entirely excusable violations. In providing these opportunities, the educational purposes and objectives of the entire program should be kept in mind.

The faulty practice of permitting absences from college classes to be made up at the rate of three or four a day during the last week in order to complete the work is to be discouraged. Intensive attendance during the last week of a term should not be allowed to replace the cumulative benefits of a normal semester's work. Regulations should provide for only a limited number of make-up periods during any week, and all students should know how many are permitted. There is little to recommend the practice of requiring two make-up periods for each absence; "one for one" is a good rule. Too many absences should automatically fail a student, even though he has a good excuse, for no one is expert enough to do passing work when he is not there. There is considerable justification in college for the practice of allowing two or three absences per semester without lowering the student's grade, provided the absence do not occur just before or just after vacation.

This makes it possible for the conscientious student who is indisposed because of a severe cold or some other ailment to refrain from class attendance and remain in bed or in his room without losing grade points. It does not provide sufficient opportunity for the malingerer to abuse the privilege.

Excuses and Substitutes

Those in charge of physical education must present in interesting, worthwhile program in order to reduce to the very minimum the excuses from physical activity and substitutes for physical activity, for quite a number of students who are excused could enjoy it if they were interested enough to want to participate. Even after the expenditure of careful effort to provide an excellent program, there will be some few students who will try to avoid physical activity classes. Besides these, there will be a limited group of students who are not able to engage in regular class work.

It is with these last two groups that we must deal concerning excuses and substitutions. It is very doubtful if anyone who is able to attend school should be excused from physical education because of some deformity, defect, of other physical handicap. Those who desire most to be excused from physical activity often need it most. Each individual's need should be met even if it be but to rest during the physical education period. However, facilities and staff are not always available to care for the few who require special treatment, and for that reason the best practical solution may be to excuse them from regular class meetings. Excuses from regular class meeting should be based on the advice of a physician, the school physician if possible.

If there is no school physician, it is best to have the examining physician fill out the school physical examination blank form, on which the specific weakness of the student is listed. This may be followed up by a conference with the physician in which he suggests types and amounts of activity that the individual may take without danger of harmful result. The physician should plan with the instructor for the student's benefit. In those cases where space and the instructor's time are available for corrective class work, this type of work, based on individual diagnosis of each student's needs, should be substituted for the normal class work; in cases where space and time are not available, the student will need to be excused from regular meetings. But in the event he is excused, he should be assigned some type of substitute work that will enable him to improve his condition or at least prevent it from getting worse.

The practice of assigning readings in hygiene to the

frail and crippled individuals who are unable to do normal class work is to be discouraged. They need modified activity or relaxation, and reading health material does not fill their need. Quite often they should read less, not more, and the instructor who increases their load is burdening them rather than building them up. The physician may recommend gentle exercise in the open for the convalescent; arm exercises for the one who is crippled; hiking for another who lost his arms; and foot exercises for on who has painful arches. These can be done outside of class if need be and reports made to the instructor. It is as reasonable, and educationally as sound, to accept reports concerning these activities as it is to accept an outline of a book in fulfilment of the requirements in physical education. To summarize briefly; excuse only in extreme cases; when it is necessary to substitute outside work for regular class meetings, provide activities that will build up rather than those that will increase the burden of the handicapped student.

Credit and Grades

The actual grade given to a class member should be awarded on an educational basis; that is, the student who most nearly attains the student attainment objectives should be given the best grade. These objectives can be grouped conveniently under the three major aspects of education and, hence, of physical education is education by means of or predominantly through the physical, rather than the education of the physical, grades given should not be based on physical skills and abilities alone but on the other two major aspects of education as well. The bases upon which grades are awarded reflect the instructor's real objectives of physical education for class work.

If one grades largely on behaviour, there is little use in denying that the attainment of discipline is the major objective; if one grades largely on strength, then the attainment of strength is the major objective; if one grades largely on skills, then the major objective is the development of skills; if one grades largely on knowledge of rules and techniques, then the attainment of this knowledge is the major objective; but, if one grades on the various social, mental, and physical aspects combined, then one is pursing well-rounded objectives of physical education.

It is useless to claim one set of objectives and operate on the basis of another, for the ones upon which one operates are the true objectives. The grade should represent degree of attainment of the objectives which have been set up for this phase of the work. It is only reasonable to grade upon the basis of what is taught in class. With the above considerations well in mind a method of grading for a class in games, where leadership opportunities are stressed, is presented. With minor modifications this same method will apply equally well to other activities and activity classes. The actual percentage of the final grade contributed by each aspect of the work will vary according to the individual instructor's philosophy.

The significant points to stress are that all aspects are included and that no one is weighted so heavily or so lightly that it is of dominant significance or of practically no significance in determining the grade. The pupils should be informed concerning the method of grading, and they should have the opportunity to check with the instructor from time to time on the progress they are making. Just how does this operate? At the first class meeting the instructor explains the purpose of the class and stresses the objectives to be pursued. He groups them under the three headings presented above and explains in some detail items that are to be included under and explains in some detail the items that are to be included under each main heading.

Under "attainment in physical aspects" he lists skills in the various games, scores on specific ability tests of speed, strength, endurance, and co-ordination, if any are to given, and other predominantly physical aspects of the class work. Under "attainment in social aspects" he lists, among others, leadership, co-operation, enthusiasm, cleanliness, self-control, sportsmanship, efficiency, and sociability. Under "attainment in mental aspects" he lists knowledge of rules, techniques, and game situations. As an aid in making clear the method of grading, he mentions specific acts or attitudes and shows how they contribute to or detract from attainment in their specific areas. When class activities start, during or after each class meeting the instructor checks under its appropriate heading any particularly worthy or unworthy performance on the part of any individual.

The record for one class period might include check because of dirty clothes for one pupil, marked enthusiasm for another, exceptionally good performance for another, lack of co-operation for another, poor choice of game element for another, and excellent leadership for another. Through the accumulation of these checks, by the end of the term some students will have many favourable marks in all three major aspects; others in some aspect; others will have few or no marks of any kind; and still others will have a number of unfavourable notated with favourable or unfavourable checks.

The great mass of average students have practically clear records. The scoring is done by code in such a way that it takes little time or space to keep the record. This record of the instructor's daily observation, then, indicates that pupil J.J.J. is very strong in attainment of the physical aspects, average in attainment of the social aspects, and slightly above average in the attainment of the mental aspects; that pupil R. E. J. is average in attainment of the physical aspects, well above average in attainment of the social aspects, and above average in attainment of the mental aspects; ant that pupil L.L.K. is practically average in all three aspects. At the end of the semester, the accumulated daily results can be totalled quickly.

These results can be supplemented by scores made on tests of physical skills and abilities; examinations on rules and game techniques, and rankings given by class members. These rankings are made without causing the students to realize that they are actually ranking themselves, in certain phases of the work. For example, when student leaders are elected a count of the votes each one gets for leader will give a fair estimate from the class of each pupil's leadership ranking by his fellows. Let us suppose five leaders are elected and each pupil votes for his five candidates. Just the five highest are leaders for the period of time involved, but the instructor can very easily keep a record of the leadership votes each pupil gets.

On another occasion it may be stimulating to present a game for some interested groups, or as final performance in some sports. By having each student vote for enough players for one team and then selecting two team on the basis of the highest total votes, the better players can be selected for this exhibition game. Here again, the instructor can keep a record of votes that each members gets, a record which represents the composite class judgment of each player's ability in that game or sport. Other opportunities of this type will present themselves to the instructor who wishes to temper his estimates of the worth of each pupil's work with the results of student estimates. The final grade will then include:

1. Attainment in social aspects:

(i) As measured by ratings of fellow students.

(ii) As measured by daily observation.

2. Attainment of mental aspects:

(i) As measured by daily observation.

(ii) As measured by tests on rules and techniques.

3. Attainment in physical aspects:

(i) As measured by tests of skills and abilities.

(ii) As measured by estimates of fellow students.

(iii) As measured by daily observation.

Concerning each aspect the instructor's daily estimate is very important. It is to a certain extent subjective, but so is every other test. Many studies have been made which show that there is little uniformity in marks given by competent teachers on written examinations in the academic school subjects. A graduate class in education, composed largely of principals, superintendents, and teachers, was given mimeographed copies of a student's arithmetic paper and asked to grade the paper. Out of this class of about seventy schoolmen the grades given on the identical mathematics paper varied from "A" to "D," and mathematics is considered and exact science. Similar results have been found concerning grading of English themes and other phases of school work. This is not a plea for avoiding exact measurement but a contention that the instructor's daily observation can hardly be less exact than results measured by some accepted types of tests. Although directly clothes are a relative matter, still the instructor knows when the pupil's clothes are dirty. He also know whether a student is antagonistic, whether he has played a game exceptionally well, or whether he is chronically late to class. If possible, measure objectively; but in the event that this is not possible, accept the fact that many subjective measures are strikingly correct and use them.

It is not possible to assign an index number of 84 or 92 or 95 to represent the affection a young man may have for a young lady in whom he is greatly interested, but by the use of subjective measurements that are available it is evident to all who see him with her that he is madly in love with her. Since our objectives cover aspects for which objective measurements are not available we would include our best subjective measures with a clear conscience. The daily observation in class of the variants from the general mean of performance in the three significant aspects is presented as on of the best and most economical subjective measures available.

Arrangement of Materials

Adequate preparation for any class meeting includes the collecting and arranging of equipment and supplies so that they will be in a convenient position for class activities. Through poor management inappreciable amount of class time can be wasted in waiting for someone to get the key to open a cabinet, to go to the equipment room for balls or bats, to place apparatus in position where it can be used, to find bases for indoor ball, to move the piano, and to perform other acts of that type. The planned lesson enables the instructor to know what materials will be needed and where they should be placed before the class starts.

It is good practice to have the class participate in moving and rearranging materials that need to be moved during the class period, but it is inexcusable practice to have most of the class wait while a few members run errands to collect materials that should have been collected ahead of class time. Insofar as class members are used in arranging equipment, they should be taught methods of doing it with accuracy and dispatch. Unless they are taught satisfactory methods of procedure, they are apt to waste considerable time stumbling through tasks that should be routine. Considerable portions of the third, fourth, and fifth class meetings can well be devoted to establishing class routine,, a part of which should include the handling, moving, and placing of materials.

Records

Only those records which are of use should be kept, for it is a waste of time to keep records for records' sake. Not infrequently, high school and universities collect numerous measurements on students and then file the information away and forget about it, partially because there is not time to do anything with it and partially because those in charge do not know how to put it to any good use.

In case of doubt a few clear records should be kept, and kept accurately and well. They should be kept on conveniently arranged forms in files or books, where they will remain clean, safe, and readily available. The following records should be kept as an aid in promoting efficient class functioning.

1. Health record. This permanent record with well have four aspects:

(a) Health inspection. A temporary record of unfavourable findings during daily inspection.

(b) Health examinations. This record should contain notations concerning defects or weaknesses of the student.

(c) Physician's recommendation. This applies to those cases for whom the physician recommends certain types and amounts of activity.

(d) Follow up. This includes notations concerning what has been done to care for defects noted above.

2. Attendance record. This should include absences and tardiness and is kept in the class grade book.

3. Record of grades given. This is kept in the grade book and shows final grade given as well as the periodic grades, which are combined to make up the final grade.

4. Record of equipment issued to class.

5. Record of locker or basket assignments This should also include combinations to lockers if combination locker are used.

6 Teacher's informational record. This is a record

for the teacher's benefit which should include a record of activities and techniques employed for the semester, with notations concerning those which were particularly successful and those which care not satisfactory. It is a very brief log of the term's work that is to serve as a guide for the next term when the work will be repeated.

7. Record of material and equipment needs.

Reports Made by the Instructor

It is essential that the administrative heads of any school know what is happening throughout their system during the school year and that they have a summary record of the significant happenings when the year is over. In order that these facts may be available for the use of those in authority, the teacher must of necessity present reports containing the desired information. The number and extent of reports will vary with the individual schools involved; in general, the larger schools will require more reports than the smaller ones. A definite effort should be made to hold the number of reports to the very minimum, and only essential material should be included. All reports should be made accurately and on time.

The fewer reports required the more time the instructor will have for each report. Much time can be saved for the teacher as well as for the office force if appropriate blank forms are used. Only a minimum of writing should be required; whenever possible, a check or some simple code figure should be used. Orderly arrangement with main heads and a few sub-heads and sufficient space to avoid crowding save time for the instructor.

Good paper should be used for the permanent report blanks, but a comparatively inexpensive grade can be used for temporary routine forms.

The instructor should make the following reports:

1. Grade report. This covers term or periodic grade as well as periodic failure report.

2. Health report. This daily report includes information concerning those who are too ill to do regular work, for those who are injured, and any cases of contagious disease.

3. Attendance report. An hourly or daily report of absences and tardiness, depending on the size and organization of the school.

4. Promotion report. This is made at the end of the term.

5. Annual report. This covers activities, particularly successful techniques, budgetary estimates, number of children participating, summary of health program, suggestions for next year, and, in general, all significant phases of instructor's work in summary form. This report can serve as an important source of information for the press and the public as well as for the administrative officers of the school.

6. Emergency report. A report concerning any unexpected circumstance or happening, especially an accident, that markedly affects class functioning. This may appear on the same blank as the health report, since it is a daily report.

Handling the Class

There are a number of people meeting physical

education classes today on the elementary, high school, and college levels who are not truly in charge of the classes they meet; in fact, no one is in charge of many of the classes. The pupils room about more or less at will and respond with delayed reaction, if at all, to the requests of the individual nominally in charge. This is due in part to an academic philosophy which maintains that personality development requires abundant self-expression. The pendulum has swung from the formal, strict-obedience type of class to one in which there is extreme freedom of action. The latter, however, has been found to have as many weaknesses as the former. Today, perhaps, in most situations, the pendulum is swinging back toward a middle position which allows more natural activities but provides instructor direction and control.

This is as it should be, for there is little use in having an instructor if the class does not respond to his wishes and plans. Student leadership and comparative freedom of action do not mean lack of instructor control, although they may indicate more remote control than is evident in strictly formal class procedure. Regulating by remote control is one of the more subtle and effective approaches in teaching activity classes; hence, it is to be recommended rather than condemned. The prime essential is that there be instructor control. Each individual has his own methods of gaining control, but there are certain fundamentals behind classes control that are worth considering, especially for use in difficult situations. Despite the fact that numerous suggestions concerning methods of class control have been written, there are still those who have disciplinary trouble, and they will continue to be with us, but perhaps in reduced numbers because of helpful suggestions and new viewpoints presented from time. The following suggestions are presented as possible aids. The instructor should:

1. Know his subject well and thus avoid embarrassing mistakes which tend to disturb one's composure and destroy confidence.

2. Remember that most of the class members want to obey most of the time and, consequently, reassure himself, when he begins to lose confidence, with the though that the majority are in accord with him.

3. Gain self-control. The individual who can control his own emotions and actions in such a way that he appears calm when he needs to appear calm, enthusiastic when he needs to be enthusiastic, and who in general has mastery of himself is well on the way toward a position of leadership before a class or in society.

4. Believe and act as though he expected the class to respond according to his wishes; have confidence, or at least the appearance of confidence.

5. Develop a sense of humour; it will carry him through many difficulties.

6. Be prompt and dependable and thus establish a routine which the class may expect. Uncertainty on the part of the pupils adds to the confusion and provides opportunities to cause trouble.

7. Meet the first challenge with determination. There are always some pupils who will try out the new instructor. A victory in the first disciplinary encounter will forestall man other incipient control problems.

8. Realize that pranks are not personal insults, and strive to treat them impersonally.

9. In case of doubt, say nothing. Many instructors have found that the use of words in handling matters of discipline follows the law of supply and demand—the more there are the less valuable each one becomes. Then too, silence is less liable to be misinterpreted than is an impromptu lecture on the behaviour of some individual or group.

In the class which starts with a short, formal routine the mechanics or arranging pupils in positions or providing for pupil movement and alignments in general must be understood if the instructor is to work efficiently. Enough formality to avoid confusion in class procedure is essential. Since it is during the first few periods that the mechanics of class movement and placement should be established, the following may well represent the activities for the first meeting on the gym floor or play area.

It is assumed that there has been one meeting before this during which the course has been discussed. When the class has collected on the activity area, it should be called together by blowing a whistle or by some other convenient means. Then the members should fall in one or two lines and arrange themselves according to height, with the tallest to the right. Since it is a good plan to have them fall in at the same place each day, they should collect at the most convenient place the first day and be asked to assemble at the same place at future meeting. After adjustments have been made so that all are in their proper places, the position of attention should be explained and practised several times. Then they should be taught the instructor's method of doing right dress

good reason for another form, the U. S. Army form might be used.

One should teach by demonstrating and explaining first and then have the students practice with corrections where needed. Then the method of taking roll should be explained, and permanent roll numbers should be assigned, after which, roll taking should be practised several times. There are some who believe that the formality suggested above is excessive—they shudder at the thought of any command response activity for fear that it will interfere with freedom of choice and action.

Some additional formality is suggested here, however, on the assumption that it is time saving and that it is more acceptable than disorganized confusion. This is recommended for purposes of efficiency and dispatch. This is not suggested for small classes of a dozen students but for larger classes, which might well be limited to forty students but for larger classes, which might well be limited to forty students, but which, in some cases, exceed one hundred.

With the purpose in mind of moving organized groups about expeditiously, some instruction in facing forward marching, and halting might well be included in the first lesson. Since each activity class period should provide stimulating exercise for all, and since class members need to get into condition as do varsity or intramural athletes, at least one third of this period should be used for more active conditioning work, which can be formal or informal according to the purposes of the class. Before dismissal the class should fall in, and roll should be taken to help establish assigned numbers and the roll-taking procedure. During the next few meetings the amount of time spent on the mechanics of class movement and on the handling of equipment and supplies should be gradually diminished and the time spent in the activities proper gradually increased as the pupils get into better condition. It is good practice to start each class with a brief period of formal lining up, dressing, roll call, and inspection, even though the remainder of class procedure is to be predominantly informal. These first few minutes should be enthusiastic and snappy, stressing alertness and exactness. In the classes with informal opening activities there are about as many procedures as there are instructors. Small classes fit well into a pattern of this type.